CLIMBING ON THE HIMALAYA

AND

OTHER MOUNTAIN RANGES

CLIMBING ON THE HIMALAYA

AND

OTHER MOUNTAIN RANGES

BY

J. NORMAN COLLIE

GYAN

Published by

Gyan Publishing House
5, Ansari Road
Daryaganj, New Delhi-110002
Phone: 011-47034999, 9811692060
E-mail: books@gyanbooks.com

Distribution Network
gyanbooks.com
India, USA, Canada, UK, Australia

ISBN: 978-93-6208-686-0 (PB)
First Published, 1902

2nd Impression 2024

Printed at: Gyan Press, Delhi.

CLIMBING ON THE HIMALAYA AND OTHER MOUNTAIN RANGES
Author: J. NORMAN COLLIE

CLIMBING ON THE HIMALAYA AND OTHER MOUNTAIN RANGES

A Stormy Sunset

CLIMBING ON THE HIMALAYA

AND

OTHER MOUNTAIN RANGES

BY

J. NORMAN COLLIE, F.R.S.

MEMBER OF THE ALPINE CLUB

EDINBURGH

DAVID DOUGLAS

1902

PREFACE

After a book has been written, delivered to the publisher, and the proofs corrected, the author fondly imagines that little or no more is expected of him. All he has to do is to wait. In due time his child will be introduced to the world, and perhaps an enthusiastic public, by judicious comments on the virtues of the youngster, will make the parent proud of his offspring.

Before, however, this much-desired event can take place, custom demands that a preface, or an introduction of the aforesaid youngster to polite society, must be written. Unfortunately also the parent has to compile a list or index of the various items of his progeny's belongings that are of interest; so that nothing be left undone that may be of service to the young fellow, what time he makes his bow before a critical audience. In books on travel, nowadays, it is customary often somewhat to scamp this necessary duty, and, after a few remarks in the preface, on subjects not always of absorbing interest, to conclude with the hope that the reader will be as interested in the description of places he has never seen as the author has been in writing about them.

Of course, formerly these matters were better managed. In the 'Epistle Dedicatorie,' the author would at once begin with :—'To the most Noble Earle'—then with many apologies, all in the best English and most perfect taste, he, under the patronage of the aforesaid Noble Earle, would launch his venture on to the wide seas of publicity, or perhaps growing bolder, would put forth his wares with some such phrases as the following :— 'And now, oh most ingenuous reader! can you find narrated many adventures, both on the high mountains of the earth, and in far countries but little known to the vulgar. Here are landscapes brought home, and so faithfully wrought, that you must confess, none but the best engravers could work them. Here, too, may'st thou find described diverse parts of thine own native land.'

'Choose that which pleaseth thee best. Not to detain thee longer, farewell; and when thou hast considered thy purchase, may'st thou say, that the price of it was but a charity to thyself, so not ill spent.'

J. N. C.

16 Campden Grove,
London, 24*th March* 1902

NOTE

Four of the chapters in this book have appeared before in the pages of the Scottish Mountaineering Club *Journal* (A Chuilionn, Wastdale Head, A Reverie, and the Oromaniacal Quest). They all, however, have been partly rewritten, so the author trusts that he may be excused for offering to the public wares which are not entirely fresh.

The Fragment from a Lost MS., and part of the chapter on the Lofoten Islands, were first printed in the *Alpine Journal.*

The author also takes this opportunity of thanking Mr. Colin B. Phillip, first, for allowing photogravure reproductions to be made of two of his pictures (The Coolin and the Macgillicuddy's Reeks), and secondly, for the great trouble Mr. Phillip took in producing the three sketches of the Himalayan mountains which are to be found in the text.

CONTENTS

LIST OF ILLUSTRATIONS

LIST OF MAPS

CHAPTER I

GENERAL HISTORY OF MOUNTAINEERING IN THE HIMALAYA

> 'Let him spend his time no more at home,
> Which would be great impeachment to his age
> In having known no travel in his youth.'
>
> SHAKESPEARE.

AT some future date, how many years hence who can tell? all the wild places on the earth will have been explored. The Cape to Cairo railway will have brought the various sources of the Nile within a few days' travel of England; the endless fields of barren ice that surround the poles will have yielded up their secrets; whilst the vast and trackless fastnesses of that stupendous range of mountains which eclipses all others, and which from time immemorial has served as a barrier to roll back the waves of barbaric invasion from the fertile plains of Hindustan—these Himalaya will have been mapped, and the highest points in the world above sea-level will have been visited by man. Most certainly that time will come. Yet the Himalaya, although conquered, will remain, still they will be the greatest range of mountains on earth, but will their magnitude, their beauty, their fascination, and their mystery be the same for those who travel amongst them? I venture to think not: for it is unfortunately true that familiarity breeds contempt.

Be that as it may, at the present time an enormous portion of that country of vast peaks has never been trodden by human foot. Immense districts covered with snow and ice are yet virgin and await the arrival of the mountain explorer. His will be the satisfaction of going where others have feared to tread, his the delight of seeing mighty glaciers and superb snow-clad peaks never gazed upon before by human eyes, and his the gratification of having overcome difficulties of no small magnitude. For exploration in the Himalaya must always be surrounded by difficulties and often dangers. That which in winter on a Scotch hill would be a slide of snow, and in the Alps an avalanche, becomes amongst these giant peaks an overwhelming cataclysm shaking the solid bases of the hills, and capable with its breath alone of sweeping down forests.

The man who ventures amongst the Himalaya in order that he may gain a thorough knowledge of

A Himalayan Camp

them must of necessity be a mountaineer as well as a mountain traveller. He must delight not only in finding his way to the summits of the mountains, but also in the beauties of the green valleys below, in the bare hill-sides, and in the vast expanses of glaciers and snow and ice; moreover his curiosity must not be confined to the snows and the rock ridges merely as a means for exercising an abnormal craze for gymnastic performances, or he will show himself to be 'a creature physically specialised, perhaps, but intellectually maimed.'

For in order to cope with all the difficulties as they arise, and to guard against all the dangers that lurk amidst the snows and precipices of the great mountains, a high standard, mental as well as physical, will be required of him who sets out to explore the Himalaya: he must have had a long apprenticeship amidst the snow-peaks and possess, too, geographical instincts, common sense, and love of the mountains of no mean order.

During these latter years few sports have developed so rapidly as mountaineering; nor is this to be wondered at, for no sport is more in harmony with the personal characteristics of the Englishman. When he sets out to conquer unknown peaks, to spend his leisure time in fighting with the great mountains, it is usually no easy task he places in front of himself; but in return there is no kind of sport that affords keener enjoyments or more lasting memories than those the mountaineer wrests from Nature in his playground amongst the hills.

Mountaineering, moreover, is a sport of which we as a nation should be proud, for it is the English who have made it what it is. There are many isolated instances of men of other nationalities who have spent their time in climbing snow-peaks and fighting their way through mountainous countries; but when we inquire into the records of discovery amongst the mountain ranges of the world—in the Alps, the frosty Caucasus, the mighty Himalaya, in the Andes, in New Zealand, in Norway, wherever there are noble snow-clad mountains to climb, wherever there are difficulties to overcome—it is usually Englishmen that have led the way.

For the pure love of sport they have fought with Nature and conquered; others have followed after; and the various Alpine Clubs which have been founded during the last twenty years are witnesses of the fact that mountaineering is now one of the pastimes of the world. It has taken its place amongst our national sports, and every year sees a larger number of recruits filling the ranks.

In one volume of that splendid collection of books which could have been produced nowhere else but in England—the 'Badminton Library of Sports and Pastimes'—we find Mr. C. E. Mathews writing: 'I can understand the delight of a severely contested game of tennis or rackets, or the fascination of a hard-fought cricket-match under fair summer skies. Football justly claims many votaries, and yachting has been extolled on the ground (amongst others) that it gives the maximum of appetite with the minimum of exertion. I can appreciate a straight ride across country on a good horse, and I know how the pulse beats when the University boats shoot under Barnes bridge with their bows dead level, to the music of a roaring crowd; and yet there is no sport like mountaineering.' This was written for a book on mountaineering, but it may be truthfully said, without making distinctions between sports of various kinds, all of which have their votaries, that a sport that demands from those who would excel in its pursuit the utmost efforts, both physical and mental, not for a few hours only, but day after day in sunshine and in storm—a sport whose followers have the whole of the mountain ranges of the world for their playground, where the most magnificent scenery Nature can lavish is spread before them, where success means the keenest of pleasure, and defeat is unattended by feelings of regret; where friendships are made which would have been impossible under other circumstances—for on the mountains the difficulties and the dangers shared in common by all are the surest means for showing a man as he really is—a sport which renews our youth, banishes all sordid cares, ministers to mind and body diseased, invigorating and restoring the whole—surely such a sport can be second to none!

But as access to the Alps and other snow ranges becomes easier year by year, the mountaineer, should he wish to test his powers against the unclimbed hills, must perforce go further afield. There are still, however, unclimbed mountains enough and to spare for many years yet to come.

In the Himalaya the peaks exceeding 24,000 feet in height, that have been measured, number over fifty,[1] whilst those above 20,000 feet may be counted by the thousand. Every year, officers of the Indian Army and others in search of game wander through the valleys which come down from the great ranges, but up to the present time only a few mountaineering expeditions have been made to this marvellous mountain land. For this there are many reasons. The distance of India from England precludes the busy man from spending his summer vacation there; the natural difficulties of the

[1] See p. 307.

country, the lack of provisions, the total absence of roads, and lastly, the disturbed political conditions, make any ordinary expedition impossible. Moreover, although the English are supposed to hold the southern slopes of the Himalaya, yet it is a curious fact that almost from the eastern end of this range in Bhutan to the western limit in the Hindu Kush above Chitral we are rigorously excluded. About the eastern portion of the Himalaya in Bhutan, and the mountains surrounding the gorge through which the Bramaputra flows, we know very little, as only some of the higher peaks have been surveyed from a distance. Next in order, to the westward, comes Sikkim, one of the few districts in the Himalaya where Europeans can safely travel under the very shadows of the great peaks. Next comes the native state of Nepaul, stretching for five hundred miles, the borders of which no white man can cross, except those who are sent by the Indian Government as political agents, etc., to the capital, Katmandu. It is evident at once to any one looking at the map of India, that Nepaul and Bhutan hold the keys of the doors through which Chinese trade might come south. The breaks in the main chain in many places allow of trade-routes, and in times gone by even Chinese armies have poured through these passes and successfully invaded Nepaul.

The idea of establishing friendly relations between India and this Trans-Himalayan region was one of the many wise and far-reaching political aspirations of Warren Hastings. On it he spent much of his time and thought. His policy was carried out consistently during the time he was Governor-General of India, and commercial intercourse during that period seemed to be well established. Four separate embassies were sent to Bhutan, one of which extended its operations to Tibet. This first British Mission to penetrate beyond the Himalaya was that under Mr. George Bogle in 1774. But on the removal of Warren Hastings from India, these admirable methods of establishing a friendly acquaintance with the powers in Bhutan and Tibet were at once abandoned. It is true that a quarter of a century later, in 1811, Mr. Thomas Manning, a private individual, performed the extraordinary feat of reaching Lhasa, and saw the Dalai Lama, a feat that to this day has not been repeated by an Englishman. But when the guiding hand and head of Warren Hastings no longer ruled India, this commercial policy sank into complete oblivion. From that day to the present little intercourse of any kind seems to have been held between the

English Government and those states in that border land between India and China.[1]

On the west of Nepaul lie Kumaon, Garhwal, Kulu, and Spiti. Through most of these districts the Englishman can wander, which is also the case with Kashmir to a certain extent.

The sources of the rivers that emerge from these Himalayan mountains are almost unknown, except in the case of the Ganges, which rises in the Gangootri peaks in Garhwal. The upper waters of the Indus, the Sutlej, the Bramaputra (or Sanpu), and the numberless rivers emerging from Nepaul and flowing into the Ganges, in almost every case come from beyond the range we call the Himalaya. Their sources lie in that unknown land north of the so-called main chain. Whether there is a loftier and more magnificent range behind is at present doubtful, but reports of higher peaks further north than Devadhunga (Mount Everest) reach us from time to time. The Indian Government occasionally sends out trained natives from the survey department to collect information about these districts where Englishmen are forbidden to go, and it is to their efforts that the various details

[1] *Narratives of the Mission of George Bogle to Tibet and of the Journey of Thomas Manning to Lhasa.* By Clements R. Markham, C.B., F.R.S. 1876.

we find on maps relating to these countries are due. Some day the lower ranges leading up to the great snow-covered mountains will be opened to the English. Sanatoria will be established, tea plantations will appear on the slopes of the Nepaulese hills, as is now the case at Darjeeling, and then only will the exploration of the mountains really begin, for which, at the present day, as far as Tibet and Nepaul are concerned, we have even less facilities than the Schlagintweits and Hooker had forty to fifty years ago.

From the mountaineer's point of view, little has been accomplished amongst the Himalaya, and of the thousands of peaks of 20,000 feet and upwards hardly twenty have been climbed. The properly equipped expeditions made to these mountains merely for the sport of mountaineering may be said to be less than half a dozen. Of course the officers in charge of the survey department have done invaluable work, which, however, often had to be carried out by men unacquainted (from a purely climbing point of view) with the higher developments of mountain craft. To this, however, there are exceptions, notably Mr. W. H. Johnson, who worked on the Karakoram range.

To omit work done by the earlier travellers, the first prominent piece of mountaineering seems to have been achieved by Captain Gerard in the Spiti district. In the year 1818 he attempted the ascent of Leo Porgyul, but was unsuccessful after reaching a height of 19,400 feet (trigonometrically surveyed). Ten years later he made the first successful ascent of a mountain (unnamed) of 20,400 feet. Speaking of his wanderings in 1817-21, he says: 'I have visited thirty-seven places at different times between 14,000 and 19,400 feet, and thirteen of my camps were upwards of 15,000 feet.' During the years 1848-49-50 Sir Joseph Hooker made his famous journeys into the Himalaya from Darjeeling through Sikkim. Obtaining leave to travel in East Nepaul, he traversed a district that since then has been entirely closed to Europeans. By travelling to the westward of Darjeeling he crossed into Nepaul, explored the Tambur river as far as Wallanchoon, whence he ascended to the head of a snow pass, 16,756 feet, leading over to the valley of the Arun river, which rises far away northward of Kanchenjunga. On the pass he experienced his first attack of mountain sickness, suffering from headache, giddiness, and lassitude. At this point he was probably nearer to Devadhunga[1] (Mount Everest) than any European has ever been, the mountain being only fifty miles away. From the

[1] Tibetan name: Jomo-kang-kar.

summit of another pass in East Nepaul, the Choonjerma pass, 16,000 feet, he no doubt saw Devadhunga. From here he returned to Sikkim, and travelled to Mon Lepcha, immediately at the south-west of Kanchenjunga. During the next year he visited the passes on the north-east of Kanchenjunga leading into Tibet and ascended three of them, the Kongra Lama pass, 15,745 feet; the Tunkra pass, 16,083 feet; and the Donkia pass, 18,500 feet. From Bhomtso, 18,590 feet, the highest and most northerly point reached by him, a magnificent view to the northward into Tibet was obtained; and Dr. Hooker mentions having seen from this point two immense mountains over one hundred miles distant to the north of Nepaul. It was during his return to Darjeeling that he and Dr. Campbell were made prisoners by the Raja of Sikkim.

During the years 1854-58 the two brothers, Adolf and Robert Schlagintweit wandered through a large portion of the Himalaya. They were the first explorers who possessed any real knowledge of snow work, having gained their experience in the Alps. Starting from Nynee Tal they followed the Pindar river to its source, just under the southern slopes of Nanda Devi. Then crossing to the north-east by a pass about 17,700 feet high, they reached Milam on the Gori river, whence they penetrated into Tibet over several passes averaging 18,000 feet. In this district, never since visited by Europeans, they made more than one glacier expedition, finally returning over the main chain, close to Kamet or Ibi Gamin (25,443 feet), on the slopes of which they remained for a fortnight, their highest camp being at 19,326 feet. An unsuccessful attempt was made on the peak, for they were forced to retreat after having reached an altitude of 22,259 feet. Returning over the Mana pass to the valley of the Sarsuti river, they descended to Badrinath. The upper valley of the Indus north of Kashmir was next explored, and Adolf, having crossed the Karakoram pass, was murdered at Kashgar.[1] In the *Journal* of the Royal Asiatic Society of Bengal (vol. xxxv.) will be found a paper by the two brothers on the 'Comparative Hypsometrical and Physical Features of High Asia, the Andes, and the Alps,' which deals in a most interesting manner with the respective features of these several mountain ranges.

In the years 1860-1865 Mr. W. H. Johnson, whilst engaged on the Kashmir Survey, established a large number of trigonometrical stations at a height of over 20,000 feet. One of his masonry

[1] Cp. *Travels in Ladâk Tartary and Kashmir*, Lieut.-Colonel Torrens, 1862, pp. 350-360, Appendix.

platforms on the top of a peak 21,500 feet high is said to be visible from Leh in Ladâk. The highest point he probably reached was during an expedition made from the district Changchenmo north of the Pangong lake in the year 1864. Travelling northwards he made his way through the mountains to the Yarkand road, and at one point, being unable to proceed, he found it necessary to climb over the mountain range at a height of 22,300 feet, where the darkness overtook him, and he was forced to spend the night at 22,000 feet. In the next year, 1865, on his journey to Khutan he was obliged to wait for permission to enter Turkestan; and being anxious to obtain as much knowledge of the country to the north as possible, he climbed three peaks—E^{57}, 21,757 feet; E^{58}, 21,971 feet; and E^{61}, 23,890 feet (?). The heights of the first two mountains have been accurately determined by a series of trigonometrical observations, but there has probably been some error made in the height of the last, E^{61}.

Mr. Johnson was a most enthusiastic mountaineer, and, owing to a suggestion made by him and Mr. Drew to the Asiatic Society of Bengal, efforts were made in 1866 to form a Himalayan Club, but through want of support and sympathy the club was never started. Mountaineering was indeed in those days so little appreciated by the political department of India that this journey of Mr. Johnson's in 1865 was made the excuse for a reprimand, owing to which he left the Service and took employment under the Maharaja of Kashmir.

About the same time that Johnson was exploring the district to the north and north-east of Ladâk, the officers of the survey, Captain T. G. Montgomerie, H. H. Godwin Austen, and others, were actively at work on the Astor Gilgit and Skardu districts. They pushed glacier exploration much further than had been done before; and it is quite remarkable how much they accomplished when one considers that in those days climbers had only just learned the use of ice-axes and ropes, and the knowledge of ice and snow even in the Alps was very limited. The exploration of the Baltoro glacier, the discovery of the second highest peak in the Himalaya—K^2, 28,278 feet—and the peaks Gusherbrum and Masherbrum, by H. H. Godwin Austen, and his ascent of the Punmah glacier to the old Mustagh pass will remain as marvels of mountain exploration.

In the next ten or fifteen years but little mountaineering was done in the Himalaya. The Government Survey in Garhwal, Kumaon, and Sikkim was carried on, and more correct maps of the mountain ranges in these parts were issued. On Kamet about 22,000 feet was reached. In Sikkim, Captain Harman, during his work for the survey, made several attempts to climb some of the loftier peaks. He revisited the Donkia pass, and, like Dr. Hooker, saw from it the two enormous peaks far away to the north of Nepaul. In order to measure their height trigonometrically, he remained on the summit of the pass (18,500 feet) all night, but unfortunately was so severely frost-bitten that ultimately he was invalided home.

In the year 1883 Mr. W. W. Graham started for India with the Swiss guide Joseph Imboden, on a purely mountaineering expedition; he first went to Sikkim, then attacked the group round Nanda Devi in Garhwal, and later returned to Sikkim and the mountains near Kanchenjunga.

This expedition of Graham's remains still the most successful mountaineering effort that has been made amongst the Himalaya. No less than seven times was he above 20,000 feet on the mountains, the three highest ascents being, Kabru (Sikkim), 24,015 feet, A^{21} or Mount Monal (Garhwal), 22,516 feet, and a height of 22,500 - 22,700 feet on Dunagiri (Garhwal). It is perhaps to be regretted that Graham did not write a book setting forth in detail all his experiences, though a short account of his travels and ascents may be found in vol. xii. of the Alpine Club *Journal*.

Arriving at Darjeeling early in 1883, he and Imboden made their way to Jongri just under Kanchenjunga on the south-west, and climbed a peak, Kang La, 20,300 feet. The Guicho La (pass), 16,000 feet, between Kanchenjunga and Pundim, was ascended, but as the end of March was much too early in the year for climbing, they returned to Darjeeling, and Imboden then went back to Europe. It was not till the end of June that Graham was joined by Emil Boss and Ulrich Kauffmann, who came out from Grindelwald. They started from Nynee Tal to attack Nanda Devi, travelling to Rini on the Dhauli river, just to the westward of Nanda Devi. From Rini they proceeded up the Rishiganga, which runs down from the glaciers on the west of Nanda Devi, but they were stopped in the valley by an impassable gorge that had been cut by a glacier descending from the Trisuli peaks. Obliged to retreat, they next attacked Dunagiri, 23,184 feet; after climbing over two peaks, 17,000 and 18,000 feet, they camped at 18,400 feet, and finally got to a point from which they could see the top of A^{22}, 21,001 feet over the top of A^{21}, 22,516 feet, and must therefore have been at least at a height of 22,700 feet. Unfortunately hail, wind, and snow drove Graham and Boss off the peak within 500 feet of the top—Kauffmann had given in some distance lower down—and it was only with difficulty that they were able to return to their camp, which was reached in the dark.

The weather then obliged them to return to Rini, from which place they again started for Nanda Devi. This time they went up the north bank of the Rishiganga. After illness, the desertion of their coolies, and all the sufferings produced by cold and wet weather, they reached the glacier in four days, only to find that again they were cut off from it by a perpendicular cliff of 200 feet, down which the glacier torrent poured. Their attempt to cross the stream was also fruitless; so, baffled for the second time, they were forced to return to their camping-ground under Dunagiri at Dunassau, from which place they climbed A^{21}, 22,516 feet, by the western ridge, calling it Mount Monal. They then tried A^{22}, 21,001 feet, but were stopped by difficult rocks after reaching a point about 20,000 feet. By the middle of August Graham was back again in Sikkim and got to Jongri by September 2. With Boss and Kauffmann he explored the west side of Kabru and the glacier which comes down from Kanchenjunga. But the weather was continuously bad; they started to climb Jubonu, but were turned back. Then they crossed the Guicho La to ascend Pundim, but found it impossible; more bad weather kept them idle till the end of the month. They then managed to ascend Jubonu, 21,300 feet. A few days later they went up the glacier which lies on the south-east of Kabru, camping at 18,400 feet; and starting at 4.30 A.M. they succeeded, owing to a favourable state of the mountain, in reaching the summit, 24,015 feet (or rather, the summit being cleft into three gashes, they got into one of these, about 30 feet from the true top). It was not till 10 P.M. that they returned to their camp. The last peak they ascended was one 19,000 feet on the Nepaul side of the Kang La. Thus ended this most remarkable series of ascents, carried out often under the most difficult circumstances. Graham, from his account of his travels, was evidently not a man to talk about all the discomforts and hardships of climbing at these altitudes, and this lack of information about his feelings and sensations above 20,000 feet has been urged against him as a proof that he never got to 24,000 feet at all. But any one who will take the trouble to read his account of the ascent of Kabru, cannot fail to admit that he must have climbed the peak lying on the south-west of Kanchenjunga, viz. Kabru, for there is no other high peak there which he could have ascended from his starting-point except Kanchenjunga itself; moreover, unless he had climbed Kabru, neither he nor Emil Boss could have seen Devadhunga nor the two enormous peaks to the north-west, which they distinctly state must be higher than Devadhunga. Now, if they climbed Kabru, they were at a height of 24,000 feet whether they had a barometer with them or not, for that is the height determined by the Ordnance Survey. The heights reached in all their other completed ascents are vouched for in the same way, for if a mountain has been properly measured by triangulation, its height is known with a greater degree of accuracy than can ever be obtained by taking a barometer to the summit.

The next real mountaineering expedition after that of Graham was in 1892, when Sir Martin Conway, together with Major Bruce, and M. Zurbriggen as guide, explored a large part of the Mustagh range. In all they made some sixteen ascents to heights of 16,000 feet and upwards, the highest being Pioneer peak, 22,600 feet.

Arriving at Gilgit in May, when much winter snow still lay low down on the mountains, they first explored the Bagrot nullah. Here they ascended several glaciers and surveyed the country. But huge avalanches continually falling entirely stopped any high climbing. They therefore went into the Hunza Nagyr valley as far as Nagyr. In the meantime, as the weather was bad, they investigated first the Samayar and afterwards the Shallihuru glaciers. At the head of the former a pass was climbed, the Daranshi saddle, 17,940 feet, and a peak called the Dasskaram needle, 17,660 feet. They then returned to the Nagyr valley and reached the foot of the great Hispar glacier, 10,320 feet. From here they travelled to the Hispar pass, 17,650 feet, nearly forty miles, thence down the Biafo glacier, another thirty miles. The Hispar pass is therefore the longest snow pass traversed outside the Arctic regions. About half way up the Hispar glacier Bruce left Conway and climbed over the Nushik La, but joined him again later at Askole.

From Askole the Baltoro glacier was ascended. Near its head the summit of Crystal peak, 19,400 feet, on the north side of the valley, was reached. From the summit, the Mustagh tower, a rival in height to K^2, 28,278 feet, was seen. To quote Conway's description: 'Away to the left, peering over a neighbouring rib like the one we were ascending, rose an astonishing tower. Its base was buried in clouds, and a cloud-banner waved on one side of it, but the bulk was clear, and the right-hand outline was a vertical cliff. We afterwards discovered that it was equally vertical on the other side. This peak rises in the immediate vicinity of the Mustagh pass, and is one of the most extraordinary mountains for form we anywhere beheld.'

Two days later they made another climb on a ridge to the east, and parallel to the one previously climbed. From here they first saw K². Amongst the magnificent circle of peaks that surrounded them at this spot, many of which were over 25,000 feet, one only seemed to offer any chance of being climbed. This was the Golden Throne. It stands at the head of the Baltoro glacier, differing greatly in form and structure from its neighbours; and of all the mountains it seemed most accessible.

Amongst, however, the enormous glaciers and snowfields that eclipse probably those of any other mountains in ordinary latitudes, even to arrive at the beginning of the climbing was a problem of much difficulty. To again quote: 'We struggled round the base of the Golden Throne, up 2000 feet of ice-fall to a plateau where we camped; then we forced a camp on to a second, and again on to a third platform . . . . we got daily weaker as we ascended . . . . we finally reached the foot of the ridge which was to lead us, as we supposed, to the top of the Golden Throne. It was an ice-ridge, and not as we hoped of snow, and it did not lead us to the top but to a detached point in the midst of the two main buttresses of the Throne.' This peak they named Pioneer peak, 22,600 feet. After this climb they returned to Kashmir.

Major Bruce, who accompanied Sir M. Conway in this expedition, has been climbing in the Himalaya for many years. In 1893, whilst at Chitral with Capt. F. Younghusband, he ascended Ispero Zorn. In July of the same year he made several ascents near Hunza on the Dhaltar peaks —the highest point reached being 18,000 feet. During August of the same year he climbed to 17,000 feet above Phekkar near Nagyr, with Captain B. E. M. Gurdon, and even in December, at Dharmsala, he had some mountaineering.

Major Bruce has done some excellent mountaineering in a district that may be said to be his alone, namely in Khaghan, a district south-west of Nanga Parbat and north of Abbottabad. Here, in company with Harkabir Thapa and other Gurkhas, a great deal of climbing has been accomplished, the district having been visited almost every year since 1894.

The best piece of climbing in Khaghan was the ascent of the most northern Ragee-Bogee peaks (16,700 feet), by Harkabir Thapa alone. This peak is close to the Shikara pass, though separated by one peak from it.

Another district visited by Major Bruce in 1898 was in Ladakh east of Kashmir—the Nun Kun range. Several new passes were traversed, and peaks up to 19,500 feet were climbed.[1]

There is certainly no mountaineer who has a record of Himalayan climbing to compare with Major Bruce's, ranging as it does from Chitral on the west to Sikkim on the east. In fact, to show how the mountains exercise a magnetic influence on him, in the summer of 1898 he saw, what no one had ever seen before, in the short space of two months, the three highest mountains in the world: Devadhunga, K^2, and Kanchenjunga.

In 1898 Dr. and Mrs. Bullock Workman traversed several passes in Ladak, Nubra, and Suru; and in 1899, with M. Zurbriggen as guide, went to Askole and up the Biafo glacier to the Hispar Pass. Then they climbed the Siegfried Horn, 18,600 feet, and Mount Bullock-Workman, 19,450 feet, both near the Skoro La. Afterwards, returning to the Shigar valley, Mount Koser Gunge, 21,000 feet, was ascended.

The last mountaineering expedition to the Himalaya was that of Mr. Douglas Freshfield, who, in company with Signor V. Sella, Mr. E. Garwood, and A. Maquignaz as guide, made the tour of Kanchenjunga, crossing the Jonsong La, 21,000 feet.

[1] *Alpine Journal*, vol. xx. p. 311.

CHAPTER II

OUR JOURNEY OUT TO NANGA PARBAT

> 'And go
> Eastward along the sea, to mount the lands
> Beyond man's dwelling, and the rising steeps
> That face the sun untrodden and unnamed.—
> Know to earth's verge remote thou then art come,
> The Scythian tract and wilderness forlorn,
> Through whose rude rocks and frosty silences
> No path shall guide thee then, . . .
> There as thou toilest o'er the treacherous snows.'
>
> R. BRIDGES.

AMONGST mountaineers, who has not at some time or another looked at the map of India, wishing at the same time for an opportunity to visit the Himalaya? to see Kanchenjunga, Devadhunga, Nanda Devi, Nanga Parbat, or any of the hundreds of snow-clad mountains, every one of which is higher than the loftiest peaks of other lands? to wander through the valleys filled with tropical vegetation until the higher grounds are reached, where the great glaciers lie like frozen rivers amidst the white mountains, while the green pasturages and pine woods below bask in the sunshine? to travel through the land where all natural things are on a big scale, a land of great rivers and mighty mountains, a land where even the birds and beasts are of larger size, a land that was peopled many centuries ago with civilised races, when Western Europe was in a state of barbarism? But these Himalaya are far away, and often as one may wish some day to start for this marvellous land, yet the propitious day never dawns, and less ambitious journeys are all that the Fates will allow. Although it had seemed most unlikely that I should ever be fortunate enough to visit the Himalaya, yet at last the time arrived when my dream became a reality. I have seen the great mountains of the Hindu Kush and the Karakoram ranges, from Tirach Mir over Chitral to K² at the head of the Baltoro glacier; I have wandered in that waste land, the marvellous gorge of the Indus. I have stopped at Chilas, one of the outposts of civilisation in the wild Shinaki country, where not many years ago no white man could venture. I have passed through the defile at Lechre, where in 1841 a landslip from the northern buttress of Nanga Parbat dammed back the whole Indus for six months, until finally the pent-up masses of water, breaking suddenly through the thousands of feet of debris, burst with irresistible force down through that unknown mountain-land lying below Chilas for many hundreds of miles, till at last the whirling flood, no longer hemmed in by the hills, swept out on to the open plains near Attock, and in one night annihilation was the fate of a whole Sikh army. Also I have seen the northern side of the mighty Nanga Parbat, the greatest mountain face in the whole world, rising without break from the scorching sands of the Bunji plain, first to the cool pine woods and fertile valleys five thousand feet above, next to the glaciers, and further back and higher to the ice-clad avalanche-swept precipices which ring round the topmost snows of Nanga Parbat itself, whose summit towers 26,629 feet above sea-level, and 23,000 feet above the Indus at its base: whilst further to the northward Rakipushi and Haramosh, both 25,000 feet high, seem only to be outlying sentinels of grander and loftier ranges behind.

It was in 1894 that the late Mr. A. F. Mummery and Mr. G. Hastings arranged that if they could obtain permission from the Indian Government to visit that part of Kashmir in which Nanga Parbat lies, they would start from England in June 1895, and attempt the ascent. Early in 1895 I made such arrangements (owing to the kindness of Professor Ramsay of London University College) that I was able to join the expedition.

We left England on June 20, joining the P. and O. steamer *Caledonia* at Brindisi. The voyage was delightful till we left Aden—even in the Red Sea the temperature never rising above 90°,—but once in the Indian Ocean we experienced the full force of the monsoon; and it was exceedingly rough from there to Bombay, which we reached on July 5. Two days later we arrived at Rawul Pindi, having had a very hot journey on the railway, a maximum of 103° being experienced between Umballa and Rawul Pindi.

At the latter place the foothills of the Himalaya were seen for the first time, rising out of the plains of the Panjab. And that night, amidst a terrific thunderstorm, the breaking of the monsoon on the hills, we slept in dak bungalow just short of Murree. From Rawul Pindi to Baramula, in the vale of Kashmir, an excellent road exists, along which one is able to travel in a tonga. These strongly built two-wheel carriages complete the journey of about one hundred and seventy miles in two or three days. Owing, however, to the monsoon rain, we found the road in many places in a perilous condition. Bridges had been washed away, great boulders many feet thick had rolled down the mountain-side sometimes to find a resting-place in the middle of the road, sometimes

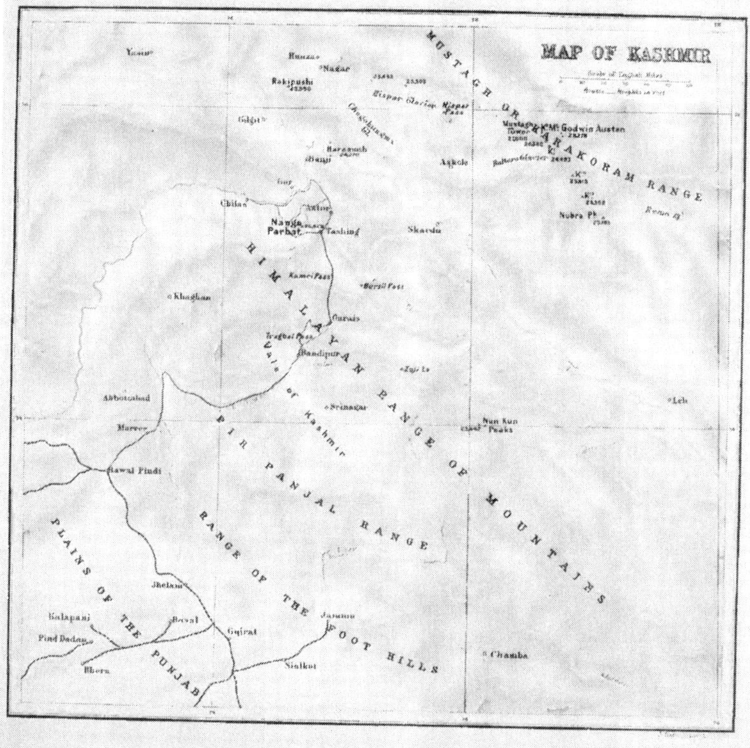

MAP OF KASHMIR
MUSTAGH OR KARAKORAM RANGE
Nazar
Rakipushi
Hispar Pass
Gilgit
Mt. Godwin Austen
Askole
Chilas
Nanga Parbat
Tashing
Skardu
HIMALAYAN RANGE OF MOUNTAINS
Kamri Pass
Burzil Post
Khaghan
Gurais
Tragbal Pass
Bandipur
Vale of Kashmir
Zoji La
Srinagar
Abbottabad
Leh
Murree
Nun Kun Peaks
Rawal Pindi
PIR PANJAL RANGE
PLAINS OF THE PUNJAB
RANGE OF THE FOOT HILLS
Jhelam
Kalapani
Pind Dadan
Gujrat
Jammu
Sialkot
Chamba
Bhera

to go crashing through it; in one place the whole mountain-side was slowly moving down, road and all, into the Jhelum river below at the bottom of the valley. But on the evening of July 9 we safely reached Baramula.

Beyond Baramula it is necessary to take a flat-bottomed boat or punt, called a dunga, traversing the vale of Kashmir by water. This valley of Kashmir, about which so much has been written, is beyond all adequate description. Situated as it is, 6000 feet above sea-level, in an old lake basin amongst the Himalaya, its climate is almost perfect. A land of lakes and waterways, splendid trees and old ruins, vines, grass-lands, flowers, and pine forests watered by cool streams from the snow ranges that encircle it, with a climate during the summer months like that of the south of France—no wonder this valley of Kashmir is beautiful.

In length about eighty miles, and twenty-five miles in breadth, it lies surrounded by giant peaks. Haramukh, 16,903 feet, is quite close; to the eastward rise the Nun Kun peaks, 23,447 feet; whilst to the north Nanga Parbat, 26,629 feet high, can be seen from the hill stations. The atmospheric colours in the clear air are for ever changing, and no better description of them can be given than one by Walter R. Lawrence in his classical work on the *Valley of Kashmir*, where as settlement officer he spent several years. He says, 'In the early morning the mountains are often a delicate semi-transparent violet, relieved against a saffron sky and with light vapours clinging round their crests. Then the rising sun deepens shadows and produces sharp outlines and strong passages of purple and indigo in the deep ravines. Later on it is nearly all blue and lavender with white snow peaks and ridges under a vertical sun, and as the afternoon wears on these become richer violet and pale bronze, gradually changing to rose and pink with yellow and orange snow, till the last rays of the sun have gone, leaving the mountains dyed a ruddy crimson, with snows showing a pale creamy green by contrast. Looking downward from the mountains, the valley in the sunshine has the hues of the opal; the pale reds of the Karéwá, the vivid light greens of the young rice, and the darker shades of the groves of trees, relieved by sunlit sheets, gleams of water, and soft blue haze, give a combination of tints reminding one irresistibly of the changing hues of that gem. It is impossible to do justice to the beauty and the grandeur of the mountains of Kashmir, or to enumerate the lovely glades and forests visited by so few.'

Nowadays Kashmir is a prosperous country. But before the settlement operations were taken in hand (1887) by Lawrence the country-people were suffering from every kind of abuse and tyranny. Now it is all changed, and under the rule of Maharaja Pratab Singh, who resolved that this settlement should be carried out and gave it his loyal support, the country-folk are contented and prosperous; the fields are properly cultivated, without fear that the harvest will be reaped by some extortionate official; the houses are rebuilt, and the orchards, gardens, and vineyards are well looked after. It was not till my return from the mountains that I had a chance of spending a few days in this fascinating valley.

After leaving Baramula our route lay for some time up the Jhelum river, which drains most of the vale of Kashmir; but soon we emerged on the Woolar lake, and in the grey morning light the hills that completely encircle the valley could be partly seen through the long streams of white mist that draped them. The lake was perfectly calm, and reflected on its surface the nearer hills. Soon we came to miles of floating water-lilies in bloom, whilst on the banks quaint mud houses and farms, encircled with poplar, walnut, and chenar trees, were visible; and, beyond, great distances of grass lands and orchards stretched back to the mountains.

But we were not across the lake. From the westward a rain-cloud was approaching, and soon the whole face of nature was changed. Small waves arose; then a blast of wind swept down part of the matting which served as an awning to our boat, and in a moment we were in danger of being swamped. The rowers at once began to talk wildly, evidently in great fear of drowning. Several other dungas, which were near and in the same plight as our own, came up, so all the boats were lashed together by ropes. Meanwhile the women and children (for the Kashmiri lives on the dunga with his wife and family) were screaming and throwing rice on the troubled waters, presumably to propitiate the evil beings who were responsible for the perilous state of affairs, and seemingly this offering to the gods was effective, for the angry deity, the storm-cloud, passed on, the wind dropped, and without further adventure we made land at Bandipur on the northern shore of the lake in warm sunshine.

Here we found ponies which had been hired for us by Major C. G. Bruce of the 5th Gurkhas. He had travelled all the way from Khaghan to Kashmir in order to engage servants, ponies, etc., and had spent a fortnight out of a month's leave in arranging these matters for us who were strangers to him. Since that time I have seen much more of Bruce, but I shall always remember this kindness. I may also say that during the whole of our expedition the military and political officers, and others whom we met, invariably helped us in every way possible.

On July 11 we loaded the ponies with our baggage and started for Nanga Parbat. Our route lay over the Tragbal or Raj Diangan pass, 11,950 feet. On the further side we descended to Kanjalwan in the valley of the Kishnganga river. Up this valley about twelve miles is the village of Gurais, where we were nearly stopped by the tahsildar, a most important village official. We wanted more ponies, which he of course promised, but next morning they were not forthcoming. Messages were useless, and seemingly persuasion also was of no avail, he assuring us that there were no ponies, and telling us every kind of lie with the utmost oriental politeness. Mummery was, however, equal to the occasion. He wrote out a telegram, which of course he never intended to send, the contents of which he had translated to the tahsildar. It was addressed to the British Resident at Srinagar, asking what should be done with a miserable official at Gurais who would give us neither help nor ponies. The effect was magical. In less than ten minutes we had three times as many ponies as we wanted, and that too in a district where everything with four legs was being pressed into the service of the Gilgit commissariat. The tahsildar rode several miles up the valley with us, finally insisting that Mummery should ride his pony, and return it after two or three days when convenient.

Just above Gurais we left the valley of the Kishnganga, and turned to the left or north-east up the valley of the Burzil. From this valley two passes lead over the range into the country that drains down the Astor nullah to the Indus: the first is the Kamri, 12,438 feet, the second the Burzil or Dorikoon pass, 13,900 feet, over which the military road to Gilgit has been made. Both these passes ultimately lead to Astor. We chose the Kamri, for we were told that better forage for our ponies could be obtained on the northern slopes. We crossed the pass on July 14, finding still some of the winter snows unmelted on the top.

From the summit we had our first view of Nanga Parbat, over forty miles away, but rising in dazzling whiteness far above all the intervening ranges. There is nothing in the Alps that can at all compare with it in grandeur, and although often one is unable to tell whether a mountain is really big, or only appears so, this was not the case with Nanga Parbat as seen from the Kamri. It was huge, immense; and instinctively we took off our hats in order to show that we approached in a proper spirit.

Two days later we camped at Rattu, where we found Lieutenant C. G. Stewart encamped with his mountain battery. He showed us the guns (weighing 2 cwt. each) which he had taken over the Shandur pass in deep snow when accompanying Colonel Kelly from Gilgit to the relief of Chitral. During this passage he became snow-blind.

The forcing of the Shandur pass was one of the hardest pieces of work in the whole of the relief of Chitral, and the moral effect produced was invaluable. For the Chitralis were under the impression that even troops without guns could not cross the pass. Imagine their consternation when a well-equipped force, together with a mountain battery, was at the head of the Mastuj river leading down to Chitral.

After we had been hospitably entertained by Lieutenant Stewart, and duly admired his splendid mule battery, we left the next day, July 16, and finally, in the dark that night, camped at the base of Nanga Parbat. During the day the ponies that we had hired only came as far as a village named Zaipur, where we paid off our men, and sent them and the ponies back to Bandipur.

We did not, however, wish to camp at Zaipur, which lay on the south side of the Rupal torrent, but were anxious to cross to Chorit, a village opposite, and then go on to Tashing. How this was to be accomplished was not at first sight very plain. But the villagers were most willing to help, and those of the Chorit village came down on the further bank, in all about fifty to sixty men. Then bridge-building began; tons of stones and brushwood were built out into the raging glacier torrent; next pine trunks were neatly fixed on the cantilever system in these piers on both sides, and when the two edifices jutted far enough out into the stream, several thick pine trunks, about fifty feet long, were toppled across, and prevented from being washed down the stream by our Alpine ropes, which were tied to their smaller ends. Several of these trunks were then placed across between the two piers, and after three hours' hard work the bridge was finished. For this magnificent engineering achievement the headmen of the two villages were presented with two rupees. We did not camp at Tashing, but crossed the glacier immediately above the village, and in a hollow amongst a grove of willows set up our tents.

We had taken twenty-seven days from London travelling continuously, but the weather was perfect. We were on the threshold of the unknown, and the untrodden nullahs round Nanga Parbat awaited us.

CHAPTER III

THE RUPAL NULLAH

'And thus these threatening ranges of dark mountain, which, in nearly all ages of the world, men have looked upon with aversion or with terror, are, in reality, sources of life and happiness far fuller and more beneficent than the bright fruitfulnesses of the plain.'—*Modern Painters.*

OUR camp in the Rupal nullah was certainly most picturesque, pitched on a slightly sloping bank of grass, strewn with wild-flowers and surrounded by a species of willow-tree which, during the hot midday sunshine, afforded most welcome shade. Firewood could be easily obtained in abundance from the dead stems and branches of the thicket, and water from a babbling stream which descended from the lower slopes of Nanga Parbat, almost within a stone's-throw of our tents.

Determined after our week's walk from Bandipur to make the most of our delightful camp, we spent the next day, July 17, in blissful laziness, doing hardly anything. We pretended now and again to busy ourselves with the tents and the baggage. A willow branch which hung in front of our tent door

A Himalayan Nullah.

would need breaking off, or a rope tightening. But the day was really a holiday, and our most serious occupation was to bask in the warm sunshine and inhale the keen, bracing mountain air fresh from the snow-fields at the head of the Rupal nullah.

The sense of absolute freedom, of perfect contentment with our present lot, blessed gift of the mountains to their true and faithful devotees, was beginning to steal over us. Languidly we talked about the morrow, our only regret arising from our inability to catch a glimpse of that monarch of the mountains, Nanga Parbat, and the ice-fringed precipices which overhang his southern face.

The Rupal is the largest nullah close to Nanga Parbat. It runs eastwards from the peaks by the Thosho pass under the whole southern face of Nanga Parbat, till it joins the valley coming down from the Kamri pass, some eight miles below Tashing. The total length is about twenty-five miles in a straight line, but only those who have wandered in these Himalayan nullahs know how that twenty-five miles can be lengthened. The interminable ups and downs, which with endless repetition confront the traveller, now descending on to glaciers by steep moraine walls, now scrambling over loose stones and debris, or crossing from one side of the nullah to the other, all the variations which a mountain path strews with such prodigality in the way, set measurement at defiance, and no man may tell the true length of a nullah twenty-five miles long. The inhabitants are wise; they speak only of a day's journey, and later we easily dropped into their ways, miles being hardly ever mentioned. In fact, to show how deceptive measurement by the map may be, when late in August we left the Diamirai nullah with the whole of our camp baggage to reach the next big nullah, the Rakiot, the traverse over two easy passes just below the snow-line took us no less than three days from early in the morning till late at night, though the distance as the crow flies is only ten miles.

Tashing, the village, which lay a few miles below us down the valley, is large and prosperous, the peasants owning many flocks and herds. Chickens, eggs, and milk are plentiful, and situated as it is some distance from the Gilgit road, any surplus stock of provisions is not depleted to the same extent as is the case with hamlets in the Astor valley. Sheep, which are small and not easy to obtain at Astor, may be purchased without difficulty at Tashing. Not many years ago Tashing used to be periodically raided by the Chilas tribesmen, who lived on the western slopes of the Nanga Parbat

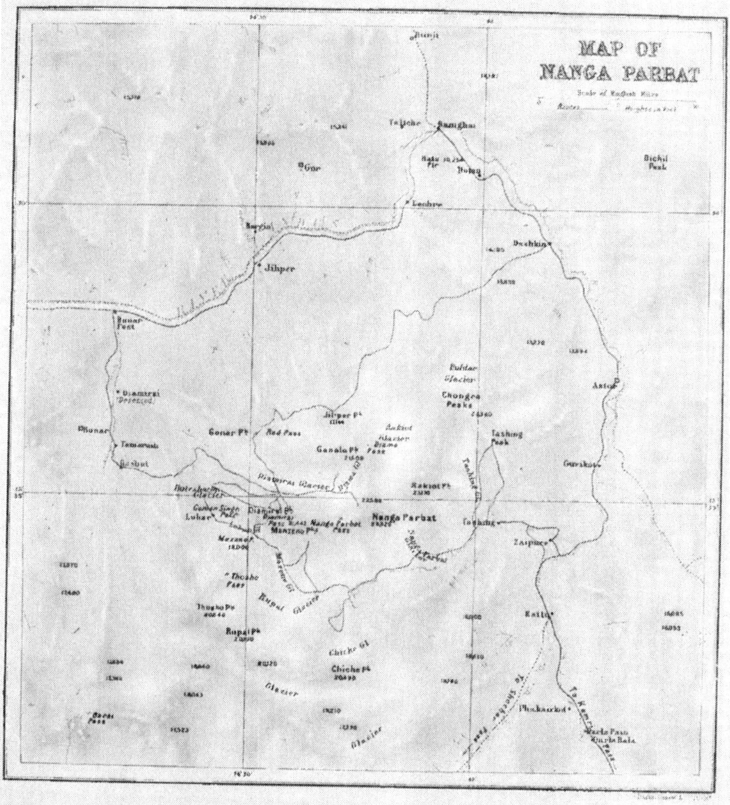
MAP OF
NANGA PARBAT
Bunji
Taliche
Bichil Peak
Gor
Jilliper
Astor
Dashkin
Chongra Peaks
Tashing Peak
Gurikot
Rakiot Pk
Ganalo Pk
Nanga Parbat
Diamirai Pk
Mazeno Pk
Rupal Glacier
Rupal Pk
Chiche Pk
Bunar
Tashing
Zaipur
Rattu
Phulwari
Diamirai Glacier
Chiche Gl
Glacier

range. They, like the old border thieves, would swarm over the Mazeno and Thosho passes and lift all the sheep and goats they could find, sometimes even taking the women as well. This, however, is now completely stopped since we 'pacified' Chilas. Mountain robbers of course still harass the land, but they have been driven further to the westward, and now it is the Chilas folk themselves who are the victims. In fact we heard later that at the end of July the tribesmen from Kohistan and Thur (to the south-west of Chilas) were pillaging the country at the head of the Bunar and Barbusar nullahs, where they had killed several shepherds and driven away their flocks.

The Rupal nullah above Tashing is fairly fertile, the vegetation stretching up a considerable distance. Pine-trees and small brushwood flourish at the foot of the Rupal or main glacier, whilst for several miles further on the north side of the valley grass and dwarf rhododendron bushes grow. The glaciers from Nanga Parbat sweep across the valley much in the same way as the Brenva glacier sweeps across the Val Véni, cutting off the upper pasturages from the villages below. Of course the highest peak in the neighbourhood is Nanga Parbat itself. But those on the south-west of the Rupal nullah, rising as they do some 7000 to 8000 feet above the floor of the valley, present a most magnificent spectacle. One especially (marked 20,730 feet) which stands alone at the head of the nullah, charms the eye with its beautiful form and exquisite lines of snow and rock. We christened it the Rupal peak, whilst its neighbour further west, almost its equal in size (20,640 feet), we named the Thosho peak.

Another summit (20,490 feet) to the eastward might, as it stands at the head of the Chiche nullah, appropriately be termed the Chiche peak, and the glacier which descends from it to the end of the Rupal glacier, the Chiche glacier. A very good idea of the relative size and form of the great main range of Nanga Parbat on the north side of the Rupal nullah may be obtained from the top of the Kamri pass. The ridge to the westward of the true summit of Nanga Parbat, stretching as far as the Mazeno La, does not culminate in any very pronounced peaks. The lowest point, probably 19,000 to 20,000 feet, lies a little over a mile directly west of the top of the mountain. We have called this dip in the ridge the Nanga Parbat pass, and two peaks marked 21,442 feet and 20,893 feet the Mazeno peaks. To the eastward of Nanga Parbat the Rakiot peak, a superb snow-capped mountain, rises to the height of 23,170 feet, and here the main ridge turns considerably more to the north-east, ending in the twin Chongra peaks, 22,360 feet, which overlook Astor and the Chongra valley. Beyond these a sudden and abrupt fall in height of about 3000 feet occurs, and the ridge running more and more in a northerly direction, and never rising above 18,000 feet in height, constitutes the western boundary of the Astor valley.

The height of our camp in the Rupal nullah was calculated from observations made with a mercurial barometer. The difference in level between the two cisterns was 531 millimetres, from which observation it was 9900 feet above sea-level.[1]

We finally decided that it would be best to obtain a good view of the south face of Nanga Parbat before we made up our minds whether we should remain in the Rupal nullah. Two of us, Mummery and I, agreed to start the next day with the intention of combining business with pleasure; in fact, we had vague ideas about climbing the Chiche peak, 20,490 feet.

[1] All the heights given, other than those taken from the Ordnance Survey, are deduced from observations made with a novel and portable form of mercurial barometer, which can be coiled up and carried in a small tin box in the pocket. As we were unable to make comparative readings with a second instrument at a known height, the barometrical readings are, in every case, calculated from the pressure at sea-level being assumed to be 30 inches. This makes the heights, as a rule, about 800 feet *lower* than if 31 inches were taken as the normal sea-level pressure.

On July 18 we set out early. Our route lay up the north side of the Rupal nullah through the fields of the small hamlet of Rupal. The morning light, the ripening crops waving in the sunshine, and the fields backed by pine woods, glaciers, and snow-peaks, were very beautiful. Unfortunately, as is usual in this part of the Rupal nullah, we were unable to obtain any view of the great peak of Nanga Parbat, our path taking us directly underneath it. Above the Rupal village the Nanga Parbat glacier sweeps across the valley from underneath the summit of the peak. This glacier, which owes its formation to avalanches perpetually falling down the southern face of the mountain, lies across the Rupal nullah almost at right angles, and forms a huge embankment varying from 500 to 800 feet high. The route up the nullah here turns off to the right, following a hollow which has been formed between the mountain-side and the true left bank of the glacier, and which we found well wooded, with a clear stream running down the centre. In all the larger nullahs the same conditions were conspicuous : usually for several miles up the valley above the end of the glacier a subsidiary valley would exist, between the side moraine of the glacier and the hill-side. These side moraines are often clothed with huge pine-trees, whilst below, birches and willows, dwarf rhododendrons and wild roses, cover the pasturages.

A climb of about 200 feet is necessary to take one on to the Nanga Parbat glacier, which at this point is flush with the top of the moraine, and, like so many others in this district, is littered with stones of all sizes. Though much more uneven, it is similar to the lower end of glaciers such as the Zmutt or the Miage. On the west side of the glacier a steep descent must be made down on to the bottom of the Rupal nullah. The floor of the valley here is carpeted with masses of brushwood. As one proceeds up the nullah two more glaciers, similar to the Nanga Parbat glacier, descend at a steep angle from the big peak, but do not stretch quite across the valley, and can be passed by walking round between their ends and the Rupal torrent. Just below the Rupal glacier itself, a well-wooded stretch of pasture-land opens out, studded with pines and other trees. Here it was that we saw, or thought we saw, our first red bear; he was some way off, but the keen-eyed shikari saw the bushes moving, and assured us that the movement was due to a 'Balu,' and as there were traces of these animals in every direction, probably the shikari was right.

Having made up our minds to camp just at the end of the Chiche glacier, we tried to effect a crossing over the Rupal torrent which looked quite shallow in several places, but these mountain streams are very deceptive. From a distance of a hundred yards nothing seems more easy than to wade across, but to any one in the swirling torrent the aspect of affairs is very different; ice-cold water with insecure and moving stones below is by no means conducive to a rapid crossing, and our shikari, who first essayed it, made but little advance. Ultimately he edged his way safely back to land, but still on the same side of the stream. Mummery, who was not to be beaten, next made a determined effort, but in his turn had to retreat after having been very nearly swept off his feet. There was, however, an alternative route. By ascending the valley to the end of the Rupal glacier a path would doubtless easily be found on the ice which would take us across to our camping-ground for the night. We were not disappointed, and soon found a spot where our tents could be pitched. The day had been more or less misty, but towards sunset the clouds began partially to roll off the peaks. Then in the gleaming gold of a Himalayan sunset we beheld the southern face of Nanga Parbat. Eagerly we scanned every ridge and glacier, as naturally we preferred to attack the peak if possible from the well-provisioned and hospitable Rupal nullah. Should we be unable to find a feasible route on this side, then it would be necessary to move our base of operations over the range into the wild Chilas country, about which we knew very little, but where we were certain supplies would be difficult to obtain. Knight, who was at Astor in 1891, writes of the Chilas country as follows:—

'That white horizon so near me was the limit of the British Empire, the slopes beyond descending into the unexplored valleys of the Indus where dwell the Shinaka tribesmen. Had I crossed the ridge with my followers, the first human beings we met would in all probability have cut our heads off.'

Our survey of the south of Nanga Parbat was not very encouraging; directly above the Rupal nullah the mountain rose almost sheer for 14,000 to 15,000 feet. Precipice towered above precipice. Hanging glaciers seemed to be perched in all the most inconvenient places, whilst some idea of the average angle of this face may be obtained from the map. The height of the glacier directly under the summit is about 11,000 to 12,000 feet—that is to say, in about two miles or *less*, measured on the map, there is a difference in height of 15,000 feet. In the Alps one can only compare it in acclivity with the Mer de Glace face of the Charmoz and

Grépon. On the south face of the Matterhorn or of Mont Blanc a mile measured on the map would probably only make a difference in height of some 5000 and 7000 feet respectively. To come to more familiar instances, the top of the Matterhorn rises 8000 to 9000 feet above Zermatt, but it is distant some six or seven miles; whilst the summit of Mont Blanc, which is 12,000 feet higher than Chamounix, is about eight miles off.

One route however seemed to offer some hopes of success. By climbing a very steep rock buttress and then traversing an ice ridge, which looked like a very exaggerated copy of the one on the Brenva route up Mont Blanc, a higher snow-field could be gained, from which the Nanga Parbat pass seemed easy of access. But as the pass was not much over 20,000 feet, at least another 6000 feet would have to be ascended, and the rocky ridge which connected it with the summit would tax the climbers' powers to the utmost. An obvious question also arose as to the possibility of pushing camps with provisions up to 20,000 feet by this route, for we were agreed that our highest camp must at least be somewhere about that altitude.

But the evening mists again drifted over the magnificent range opposite and soon hid the upper part of the mountain. They did not finally disappear till long after sunset. In the meantime we contented ourselves with planning our expedition for the morrow by the light of the camp fire. The height of the camp by mercurial barometer was 12,150 feet.

Before daylight next day we started up the middle of the Chiche glacier, accompanied by two of our Kashmiri servants. Stones without number covered the ice, and our lanterns only sufficed to show how unpleasant our path on the glacier was likely to prove. Soon the cold grey of the morning revealed the Chiche peak straight in front of us, a dim and colourless shadow. Quickly the dawn rose; we saw the bare precipitous ice slopes on its northern face, scored everywhere by avalanche grooves, and the loneliness of the scene impressed itself upon us. We were entering on a new land, a country without visible trace of man; probably we were the first who had ever ventured into its recesses. No breeze stirred, and the eastern sun slanting across the peaks threw jagged shadows over the snows; soon rising higher in the heavens, it topped the ridges and bathed us in its warm glow.

At once the glacier wakened into life, and as the stones on the surface were loosened from the frozen grip of night, those which were insecurely perched would ever and again fall down the slippery ice;

then would we hear a grating noise followed by a deep thud or booming splash. These luckless stones had 'left the warm precincts of the cheerful day,' and deep in the cavernous hollows of each crevasse or below the still green water of the glacier pools they rested, till such time as the crushing heel of the relentless ice should grind them slowly to powder.

Grand and solemn in the perfect summer's morning was my introduction to the snow world of the mighty Himalaya. The great hills were around me once more. The peaks, ridges, ice-clad gullies, and stupendous precipices encircling me, sent the blood tingling through my veins; I was free to climb where I listed, and the whole of a long July day was before me. To those whose paths lie in more civilised and inhabited regions, this enthusiasm about wild and desolate mountains may seem unwarranted, may, perhaps, even savour of an elevation of fancy, a vain belief of private revelation founded neither on reason nor common sense. They probably will agree with Dr. Johnson, who writes of the Western Highlands of Scotland: 'It will readily occur that this uniformity of barrenness can afford little amusement to the traveller; that it is easy to sit at home and conceive rocks, heaths, and waterfalls, and that these journeys are useless labours which neither impregnate the imagination nor inform the understanding.' The 'saner' portion of humanity, on the whole, are of one mind with the great Doctor, at least if one can judge from their utterances, and the votary of the mountains is often looked upon with pity as one who, being carried away by a kind of frenzy, is hardly responsible for his actions.

A sport like mountaineering needs no apology. Moreover, it has been so often and so ably defended by writers with ample knowledge of their subject, that nothing remains for me to say to this 'saner portion,' unless perhaps I might be allowed to quote the following oracular remark: '"But it isn't so, nohow," said Tweedledum. "Contrariwise," continued Tweedledee, "If it was so it might be; and if it were so it would be; but as it isn't, it ain't. That's logic."'

There are, however, those who accuse the mountaineer of worse things than a foolish and misguided enthusiasm about the waste places of the earth. I have often been told that this ardent desire for wild and rugged scenery is an unhealthy mental appetite, the result of the restless and jaded palate of the age, which must be indulged by new sensations, no matter at what cost. Why cannot the mountaineer rest content with the fertile valleys, the grass-clad ranges, and the noble forests with the streams flashing in the sunlight? Why cannot he be satisfied with these simpler and more homely pleasures? To what end is this eagerness for scenes where desolation and naked Nature reign supreme, where avalanches thunder down the mountain-sides, where man has never lived, nay, never could live?

To a few the knowledge of the hills is given. They can wander free in the great snow world relying on their mountain craft; and should their imagination not be impregnated nor their understanding informed, then are their journeys indeed useless. For Nature spreads with lavish hand before them some of the grandest sights upon which human eye can gaze. Delicate, white, ethereal peaks like crystallised clouds send point after point into the deep azure blue sky. Driven snow, marvellously moulded in curving lines by the wind, wreathes the long ridges; and in the deep crevasses the light plays flashing backwards and forwards from the shining beryl blue sides: sights such as these delight the soul of the mountaineer and tempt him always onward.

The ever-varying clouds, forming, dissolving, and again collecting on the mountains, show, here a delicate spire of rock, undiscernible until the white curling vapour shuts out the black background, there a lesser snow-peak tipped by the sunlight floating slowly across it and rimmed by the white border of the morning mists.

But it is needless for the lover of the mountains to describe these sights; the mere stringing together of word-pictures carries little conviction. The sailor who spends his life on the ocean might just as well attempt to awaken enthusiasm for a seafaring life in the minds of inland country-folk, by describing the magnificence of a storm at sea, when the racing waves drive by the ship and the wind shrieks in the rigging, or by telling them of voyages through summer seas when the fresh breezes and the long rolling billows speed the ship on its homeward way through the ever-changing waters.

The subject, however, must not be taken too seriously. No doubt the average individual has most excellent reasons for abstaining from climbing hills, whilst the mountaineer is, as a rule, more competent to ascend peaks than to explain their attractions; and to quote from a fragment of a lost MS.,[1] probably by Aristotle: 'Now, concerning the love of mountain climbing and the excess and deficiency thereof, as well as the mean which is also a virtue, let this suffice.'

But I have wandered far from the Chiche glacier.

[1] Cp. page 304.

Whether it was owing to our tremendous burst of enthusiasm which reacted on our ambition, or to a lack of muscle necessary for a hard day's work, nevertheless it must be recorded that presently our anxiety to climb the Chiche peak gradually dwindled, and after several tentative suggestions we both eagerly agreed that from a smaller summit just as good a view of Nanga Parbat could be obtained as from one 20,490 feet high.

We therefore turned our attention to a spur on our right which ran in a northerly direction from the Chiche peak. As the day wore on even this proved too much for us, and after tediously floundering through soft snow, and cutting steps up a small couloir of ice, a strange and fearsome process to our Kashmiris, we sat down to lunch, at a height of 16,000 feet, and basely gave up any ideas of higher altitudes. We were hopelessly out of condition. Below us on our left lay a most enticing rock ridge, where plenty of fun and excitement could be had, and from its precipitous nature in several places, it would evidently take us the rest of the afternoon to get back to our camp.

Clouds persistently interfered with the view of Nanga Parbat, but now and again its summit would shine through the drifting vapours, showing precipice above precipice. The eastern face of the

Chiche peak, which we saw edgeways, was superb. Nowhere in the Alps is there anything with which one can compare the savage black corrie which nestled right in the heart of the mountain, showing dark, precipitous walls of rock, with here and there a shelf where isolated patches of snow rested. This corrie forms one of the heads of the Chiche nullah, which would be worth visiting for this solitary and savage view alone. As we descended our rock-ridge we had to put on the rope, and soon experienced all the pleasures of the initiated. Our bold and fearless Kashmir servants got more and more alarmed; and the peculiar positions they occasionally thought it necessary to assume made us feel how sweet is the joy of being able to accomplish something that an inexperienced companion regards as impossible. In many places it was only by very great persuasion that they were induced to move. Many were the things they told in Hindustani, which we understood but imperfectly, though we gathered in a general way that no self-respecting Kashmiri would ever attempt to climb down such places, and that even the ibex and markhor would find it an impossibility, a true enough assertion, seeing that many of the small rock faces to be negotiated were practically perpendicular for fifteen or twenty feet.

We reached our tents late in the afternoon to find that Hastings had come up from the lower camp. A council of war was then held. Evidently we were not in condition to storm lofty peaks; and in order to get ourselves into proper training, a walk round to the other side of Nanga Parbat was considered necessary. Hastings as arranged had brought up plenty of provisions, thus enabling the party to brave the snows and uninhabited wilds in front of them. Our immediate movements decided upon, we sat round the camp fire, dined, smoked, talked, and finally, when the stars were shining brightly above the precipice-encircled summit of Nanga Parbat opposite, retired into our sleeping-bags for the night.

CHAPTER IV

FIRST JOURNEY TO DIAMIRAI NULLAH AND THE DIAMIRAI PASS

> 'Lo! where the pass expands
> Its stony jaws, the abrupt mountain breaks,
> And seems, with its accumulated crags,
> To overhang the world.'
>
> SHELLEY.

EARLY the next morning, before the sun had risen, we started for the Mazeno La, which should lead us into the wild and unknown Chilas country. We soon experienced the kind of walking that afterwards we found to be more often than not the rule. Loose stones of every size and description lay piled between the edge of the glacier and the side of the valley, and it was useless to attempt to walk on the glacier itself, for not only was it buried deep with debris, but was crevassed as well. For some distance we followed the northern or left bank, passing by the snout of a small ice-fall that came down from the main range of Nanga Parbat, and then turned to the right up and over an intervening spur, which finally brought us to the level of the glacier that lay immediately under the Mazeno La. Across this our path lay in the burning sun of the morning. Before us, about 1500 feet higher up, was the pass; first the glacier was crossed, and then partly by rocks and partly over soft snow the way led upwards. Within a few hundred feet of the summit (18,000 feet) I experienced a violent attack of mountain sickness, and was hardly able to crawl to the top. This was the only time any of the party suffered at all, and later a slight headache or lassitude was the only symptom that I ever felt, even when at heights up to 20,000 feet.

The western face of the pass is much more precipitous than the one we had ascended, but by making use of an easy rock arête we soon got down (2000 feet) to the more level glacier below. The Mazeno La on the western side somewhat resembles the Zinal side of the Triftjoch, but is not quite so difficult.

The more active of our coolies, together with servants, were sent on with the instructions to camp on the right-hand side of the glacier as soon as they should come to any bushes out of which a fire could be made, but we were not destined that evening to camp in any comfort. Caught on the glacier by the darkness we were forced to sleep for the night on a small plot of grass on the edge of the side moraine, 13,400 feet, and not till the next morning did we rejoin our coolies about a mile and a half lower down the valley. After we had obtained sufficient to eat we started down beside the glacier, which I have named the Lubar glacier on account of the small shepherds' encampment of that name just below the end of it. On our arrival at Lubar we made our first acquaintance with the Chilas folk, some of whom looked very wild and unkempt, but throughout our expedition we found them to be friendly enough, and never experienced any difficulty with them. Some sour and particularly dirty goats' milk out of huge gourds was their offering to us, and a small sheep, price four rupees, was purchased.

Our destination, however, was the Diamirai nullah on the north-west of Nanga Parbat, so we did not stay long, and winding away up the hill-side, leaving the Lubar stream far below us on the left, we first traversed a beautiful wood of birch-trees, and later got out on to the bare hill-side.

Only two small ridges separate the Diamirai from the Lubar nullah, but they are only small in comparison with their bigger neighbours; consequently we did not reach the Diamirai nullah that day, but camped on the hill-side by a small stream at

12,500 feet. A magnificent view to the west showed all the country stretched out before us, a country untravelled by any European, whilst skirting the horizon were some splendid snow-peaks that lay near the head of the Swat valley beyond Tangir and Darel. Next day, July 22, before coming to the Diamirai nullah a herd of markhor was seen on the slope not far in front of us, and by midday we camped on the south side of the huge Diamirai glacier that fills up the centre of the nullah, having taken about five hours from our last camp, and having come over some very rough ground. As soon as the baggage was unpacked it was discovered that a pair of steig-eisen had been left at the camp of the night before. One of the goat-herds from Lubar had come with us, and he, being promised a rupee should he bring them back, started at about two o'clock, running up the hill-side like a goat, and by half-past six o'clock was back again with them. Of course, these men having been trained in the hills are very agile, and able to cover long distances, but considering the height there was to climb, and the nature of the ground traversed, his was a fine performance.

The camp (12,450 feet) was placed amongst some stunted pine-trees and huge boulders that had rolled down the moraine, the glacier itself being high (200 feet) above the floor of the valley at the side.

The view to the westward was much the same as we had seen the night before, only with this difference: it was enclosed now between the two sides of the Diamirai nullah, whilst the glacier fell away down the valley in the foreground, towards the Indus, 10,000 feet below. Beyond, range after range receded to the horizon, the furthest peaks probably being more than one hundred miles distant. There the mountain thieves of Darel, Tangir, and of the country west of Chilas live unmolested.

But eastward, at the head of the valley, towered Nanga Parbat, 14,000 feet above us, one mass of ice and snow, with rock ribs protruding here and there, and vast overhanging glaciers ready at any moment to pour down thousands of tons of ice on to the glaciers below. Lit up a brilliant orange by the setting sun, and with the shadows on the lower snows of a pale green, it certainly looked most beautiful, but up its precipitous face a way had to be found, and at first sight it did not look very promising.

From our camp we could see the whole face, and Mummery was not long before he pointed out a route by which we hoped later to gain the upper snow-fields just underneath the summit, and thence the topmost pinnacle which glistened in the sunlight.

The provisions brought over from the Rupal nullah were only meant to last for a few days, so, after the exploration of the western side of Nanga Parbat, it became necessary to arrange for the return. The servants and coolies were sent back by the route we had come, whilst we made up our minds to cross the ridge on the south side of the valley sufficiently high up to bring us down either on to the Mazeno La, or, if we were fortunate, into the head of the Rupal nullah.

I went for a walk about four miles up the glacier, but was unable to find a break in the great wall at the head of the Diamirai nullah. On my return I nearly ran into the arms of a huge red bear; and I must confess that we both were very much frightened.

That night, a little before midnight, we started with lanterns, picking our way first through the small rhododendron bushes by the side of the glacier for about a mile, then turning to the right obliquely up the hill-side with the intention of reaching a rock rib which led up to a gap in the great wall that bounded the Diamirai nullah on the south side. For a long time we stumbled up

The Diamerai Pass from the Red Pass

what seemed an interminable shoot of loose stones, but by the time the early dawn gave sufficient light to enable us to see where we were, a rock arête came into view on our left.[1] Towards this we made our way, finding the climbing was by no means difficult. Occasionally the arête would become too perpendicular for us to follow it, and then we had to cut steps along the top of ice- or snow-slopes that were underneath the rocks on the top of the ridge and chance finding our way back up some gully or subsidiary rib of rocks that might branch out from the main arête.

We did not seem to waste much time, but long after the sun had risen and the silent ranges of blue mountains had flushed first with the rosy tints of the rising sun and afterwards glistened with the full blaze of the morning, the pass was still far away above us. These Himalaya are constructed on a totally different scale from either the Alps or any of the ordinary snow mountains. Still, point after point had to be surmounted. Once in the mist that settled down on us about eleven o'clock, we at last thought the summit was reached, and began to descend an arête that led towards the south. Twenty minutes later, when it cleared, great was our vexation to find the pass

[1] See illustration facing page 90.

still a long distance above us on our right, and that we had unconsciously been descending towards the Diamirai nullah. Upwards again we had to climb, finally finding that the ridge led to the top of a peak on the west of the pass and about a thousand feet higher. In order to save the extra fatigue of climbing to the summit and again descending to the pass, Mummery made a bold effort, striking across the face of the mountain. In some places rocks stuck out from the steep face, in others ice slopes had to be crossed, and towards the middle a great circle of soft snow, with steep ice underneath, gave us an anxious time; for should the surface snow have avalanched away, it would not have stopped for certainly several thousand feet. By tying two ropes (eighty and sixty feet long) together, we spread ourselves out as far apart as possible, and very carefully made our way across. It was two in the afternoon before the summit of the pass was reached; its height was 18,050 feet. We have named it the Diamirai pass. Mummery assured us that he had never been over a more sporting pass, and we were delighted with the varied climbing that we had experienced. But our enthusiasm was soon checked; below, on the further side, we could see neither the wished-for Rupal nullah nor the Mazeno La. Easy rocks and snow led down to a small glacier, which, flowing southwards, led into another and larger glacier whose trend was to the west. Evidently the larger glacier was the Lubar. The position we were in gradually began to dawn on us. In fourteen hours we had made, as the crow flies, three miles; of course we had climbed about six thousand feet, but in front of us lay a descent of three thousand feet, and on to the wrong side of the range, therefore at least five miles away round the corner on the left was the Mazeno La, 18,000 feet. We also knew that our camp, and probably our first food, was nearly twenty miles on the other side of the Mazeno, and to make matters worse we had only a few scraps left, a slice of meat, some sticks of chocolate, and about half a dozen biscuits. There was no time to admire the view, also not much view to admire, for the customary midday mists completely hid Nanga Parbat and all the higher peaks. As an heroic effort Mummery suggested that it might save time to climb up from the pass on the south side, over a peak nearly 21,000 feet, in order to drop down on to the Mazeno La; but we soon decided that it was imprudent so late in the day to attempt it, especially as it would most certainly involve spending the night out at some very high altitude. We therefore rapidly descended the easy slopes on the south side of this pass, to which, as I have said, we gave the name of Diamirai. After running down the foot glacier, the Lubar glacier was reached at about half-past five. Here we stopped and rested for about an hour and a half, vainly attempting to get away from a bitterly cold wind that was blowing up from the west. But there was no shelter, so the lesser of two evils was chosen, namely to go on. Slowly we crawled to the foot of the Mazeno La, and about twenty hours after we had started on our expedition, without food, and with only the light of our lanterns, we toiled up the slopes that would bring us at last to the top of our second pass, 18,000 feet above sea-level. I shall never forget how tobacco helped me through that night, as I smoked whilst waiting on the summit, in the freezing air and the bright starlight, for Mummery and Hastings; it almost made me feel that I was enjoying myself; and it stayed the pangs of hunger and soothed away the utter weariness that beset both mind and body.

During our wild nocturnal wanderings, first down the Mazeno, and then down the Rupal glacier, where in the dim candle-light and in a semi-conscious condition we slipped, tumbled, and fell, but always with one dominant idea—namely, we must go on!—that pipe continued to help me. What cared I though Hastings growled?—he does not smoke!—or whether poor Mummery groaned aloud as he stepped into icy pools of water. So we stumbled frantically forwards, over the vast wilderness of stones and ice; and I remember, as we groped our way onwards, I must have half fallen asleep, for I could not get out of my mind that there was a hut or a small hotel on the top of the Mazeno La, and that for our sins we had been doomed to wander for ever in this dismal and waste land of cold and darkness, whilst rest and food were foolishly left behind.

But daylight came at last, and, after the sun was well up in the sky, we finally made our way off that dreadful glacier. We also had vague hopes that perhaps after all we might be able to get something to eat before we reached our camp, miles away near Tashing. For one of our Kashmiri servants had been told to wait at the foot of the glacier—a week if necessary—till we turned up. We were quite uncertain whether he would follow our instructions, but at seven o'clock Hastings and I found him camped under a huge rock. At once some provisions and a kettleful of hot tea were sent back to Mummery, who was resting some miles up the valley. At half-past ten I left Hastings and Mummery asleep amongst the flowers in the shade under the rock, and set off alone for the lower camp, if possible to hurry up some ponies to fetch them down the valley. Early in the afternoon I met them with two of the Rupal coolies: they had crossed the Nanga Parbat glacier, no easy thing to do, but, the steep face of dried mud and boulders about thirty feet high leading off the glacier, they could not get up. Engineering operations at once became necessary; with my ice-axe I cut large footsteps diagonally upwards across this steep face. But the first pony was afraid. After some talking, one of the men led up a wise-looking, grey pony to the bottom, and, talking to it, showed it the staircase. It then climbed up, feeling each step carefully with its forelegs before venturing on to it. These unshod mountain-horses are certainly extremely clever on such kind of ground. Several years later, when travelling in the Canadian Rocky Mountains with a whole pack of Canadian ponies, a place not one-quarter as difficult entirely stopped the whole outfit, although for making their way through fallen timber and across dangerous streams these Canadian ponies are unequalled.

Between five and six that evening I arrived at our Tashing camp and found Bruce there. He had obtained a month's leave, bringing with him two Gurkhas—Ragobir and Goman Singh. Over our dinner we forgot the weary tramping of the last forty hours, celebrating the occasion by drinking all the bottles of Bass's pale ale—a priceless treasure in these parts—that we had brought from Kashmir. Then afterwards, when we turned into our sleeping-bags before the roaring camp-fire, and the twilight slowly passed into the azure night, and overhead the glistening stars were blazing in the clear sky, a worthy ceiling to this mountain land, it was agreed unanimously that it was worth coming many thousand miles to enjoy climbing in the Himalaya, and that those who lived at home ingloriously at their ease knew not the joys that were to be found amidst the ice and snows of the greatest of mountain ranges. Never would they enjoy the keen air that sweeps across the snow-clad heights, never would they wander homeless and supperless over the vile wastes which surround the Mazeno La for the best part of two nights and two days; and, last but not least, never would such joys as the marvellous contentment born of a good dinner, after incipient starvation, nor the delicious rest that comes as the reward after excessive fatigue—never would joys such as these be theirs.

CHAPTER V

SECOND JOURNEY TO DIAMIRAI NULLAH AND ASCENT TO 21,000 FEET

> 'And this, the naked countenance of earth,
> On which I gaze, even these primæval mountains,
> Power dwells apart in their tranquillity,
> Remote, serene, and inaccessible.'
>
> SHELLEY.

NEXT day Bruce and I with Ragobir and Goman Singh went for an excursion up the Tashing glacier, in order that the two Gurkhas might have some experience in ice-work and step-cutting. It was great fun, and although I was perfectly unable to understand any of their conversation, Ragobir and Goman Singh were laughing, chattering, and playing the whole time like two children.

On July 27 the same party, with the addition of Mummery, started for a ridge which runs south-east towards Tashing from the peak marked 22,360 feet, which we named Chongra peak, as it is at the head of the valley of that name above Astor. We crossed the Tashing glacier, and camped at 15,000 feet by some rocks. Next day was spent in a ridge-wander. Our intention was to climb a rock peak overlooking the Chongra nullah; but laziness was in the air, the day was hot, and the ridge endless. Finally a halt was called somewhat short of the peak that we had intended to climb, and for a long time we basked in the sun, smoked, ate our lunch, and enjoyed the superb view of the precipices of Nanga Parbat on the west and of the Karakoram range far away to the northward. Out of the masses of snow-clad giants in the remote distance to the north-east, one rose obviously higher than all its neighbours; in shape it resembled the view of K^2 as seen from Turmik.[1] Since then, however, Bruce has told me that the mountain that was seen from Turmik was probably the Mustagh tower. These two peaks would be about one hundred miles away, and in that clear atmosphere should be perfectly visible from our position (about 17,000 feet), for we were high enough to see over the range on the east of the Astor valley. We also saw across the Indus and up the Shigar valleys, and further

[1] In Drew's *Jummoo and Kashmir Territories*, p. 370, also *Alpine Club Journal*, vol. xvii. p. 38, there is a sketch showing a mountain supposed to be K^2. Drew also has drawn K^2 in No. 3 Isometric view of the mountains on the north-east of the Indus river. When Drew made these sketches the existence of the Mustagh tower, which rivals K^2 in height, was unknown; moreover both from Turmik, and also from near Gilgit where the Isometric view No. 3 was taken, the Mustagh tower would be almost exactly in front of K^2.

still the eye was directed straight up the Baltoro with no high peaks or ranges to intercept its view. Very much nearer and more to the north just on the other side of the Astor nullah a really magnificent double-headed peak, the Dichil,[1] sends up a series of perfectly impossible precipices. Its height on the map is 19,490 feet, but I am positive this measurement must be wrong. Much later, whilst returning from the Rakiot nullah to Dashkin, I was at a point 16,000 feet on the ridge just opposite across the Astor valley, and seen from there it apparently towered at least 5000 feet above me. In the Dichil nullah at its foot the valley cannot be more than 10,000 feet, and the view of it from this nullah must far surpass that of Ushba in grandeur.

During the day a curious haze hung over some of the precipices at the head of the Tashing glacier just opposite to us, due to perpetual avalanches of stones which were partly falling, partly sliding, down the steep slopes.

We returned to camp by a different route. A steep rock ridge led straight down from the peak we were on to the Tashing glacier below. On this ridge we had some delightful climbing, ultimately

[1] There is a drawing of this peak on page 119 of Sir W. M. Conway's *Climbing in the Himalaya*.

reaching the upper pasturages lying on the left bank of the glacier. It was a long tramp from there home, but just as it became dark we marched into our camp beneath the grove of willows.

The 29th was spent preparing for our start for the Diamirai nullah, for Mummery had quite given up all idea of attempting to climb the thousands of feet of almost perpendicular wall that ran the whole way along the south face of Nanga Parbat. The next day we started with a perfect caravan of coolies. Our intention was to send Goman Singh and our servants, together with all the coolies and baggage, over the Mazeno La by the route we had first taken, whilst we ourselves with Ragobir should try to cross directly from the head of the Rupal nullah to the head of the Diamirai nullah.

This time we hoped to have better luck than on our return over the Diamirai pass. But it was with some misgiving that I started, for I alone in my walk a week before up the Diamirai glacier had seen the head of that nullah, and although I did not doubt that we might reach the head of some pass from the southern side, I could not remember any place where it would be possible for us to descend on the northern side, and under any conditions our pass would be at least 20,000 feet, probably more, for the route lay directly over the spur which leads westward from the summit of Nanga Parbat to the Mazeno La. That night we camped about four to five miles short of the Mazeno La at a height of 13,000 feet. In the dark we started next morning up excessively steep and broken moraine by the side of an ice-fall, thence we turned on to the steep glacier, and after some difficulty got on to the upper glacier, which came down from the north-east. After following this for some distance we turned to our left up a wide couloir, and partly on rocks and partly on snow slowly climbed upwards. By three in the afternoon Bruce, who was not in such good condition as we were, and was suffering from suppressed mumps (although neither he nor we knew it at the time), began to feel tired, but under the stimulation produced by some citrate of caffeine lozenges he went on again bravely. At last we came out on to the ridge at the head of the couloir, and climbed some few hundred feet up the arête, which seemed to lead to the very summit of the peak marked 21,442 feet on the map. But the time was five o'clock in the afternoon. The height by mercurial barometer was 20,150 feet. We had climbed over 7000 feet; but beyond feeling very tired, which was natural, we were hardly affected by the rarefied air. Here we stopped for some short time

The Mazeno Peaks from the Red Pass.

and had our evening meal. Bruce and I came to the conclusion that, as we must certainly spend the night out somewhere, a less exalted position was preferable. We selected a new route, which would take us down to the foot of the Mazeno La, Ragobir coming with us. Mummery and Hastings would not hear of beating a retreat thus early, so they arranged to go on, and should they find the ridge become too difficult further up, they would return and follow us down, but they hoped for a full moon and the possibility of climbing on during the night.

Bruce and I did not make much progress, for our ridge soon became both narrower and more precipitous; but finally, as the sun was setting, we found a crack running through the arête into which a flat stone had got jammed just large enough for three people to sit on. Here we made up our minds to stop for the night. Roughly we were 19,000 feet, or 1000 feet higher than the Mazeno La, and about two to three miles to the eastward of it. A stone thrown out on either side of our small perch would have fallen many hundreds of feet before hitting anything, so we did not take off the rope, but huddled together as best we could to keep warm.

I could write a very long description of the wonderful orange sunset we saw beyond the Mazeno, how the light faded out of the sky, and the stars came out one by one as the sunset disappeared; how we tried in vain to get into positions such that the freezing wind would not penetrate our clothes, how Bruce and Ragobir groaned, and how we suffered—but I will refrain. Let any one who may be curious on the subject of a night out on a rock ridge at 19,000 feet try it; but he must place himself in such a position that, twist and turn as he may, he still encounters the cold, jagged rocks with every part of his body, and though he shelter himself ever so wisely, he must feel the wind steadily blowing beneath his shirt.

Late in the night we heard noises on the ridge above us. It was Mummery and Hastings returning. But, although they were within speaking distance of Bruce and myself, and I had lit a lantern to show them where we were, they could not reach us, and finally had to select the least uncomfortable place they could. With leaden feet the night paced tardily on, and brilliant stars and moon that had at first shone from the zenith gradually sank towards the west, but how slowly!—

> 'Yon lily-woven cradle of the hours
> Hath floated half her shining voyage, nor yet
> Is by the current of the morn opposed.'

Would the morning never come, and with it the warm sunshine? Daylight crept up the sky, however, at last, and as soon as they could, Mummery and Hastings joined us. After we left them, they had climbed some considerable distance further, but as the mists did not lift at sundown and the other side of the range was unknown, they perforce had to return, having nearly reached the summit of the mountain and a height of 21,000 feet. It was a long time before we got down on to the Mazeno glacier, but somewhere about ten o'clock we arrived on the flat glacier. Here the party, overcome by the warmth of the sunshine and a great drowsiness, went to sleep on some of the flat slabs of stone that lay scattered on the ice. Personally, nothing would have given me more pleasure than to have followed the example of the rest, but visions of another night out on the Lubar glacier troubled me. Moreover, we had nothing whatever to eat, the night before having seen the last of our provisions. Ragobir and I therefore with weary feet started to cross the Mazeno La.

Very slowly we toiled and toiled upwards through the already softened snow; but long before we reached the summit, more than once Ragobir had lain down on the ground exhausted. I found out later that he had eaten nothing whatever the day before. Ultimately we got to the top and rested awhile. Our mission was to get to Lubar, and from there send back up the glacier milk and meat to the remainder of the expedition. It was already mid-day, and here was I with a Gurkha who could hardly crawl, and the rest of the party perhaps in a worse condition far behind. So after a short rest, I started down from the pass on the west side, soon leaving Ragobir behind. Then I waited for him. Repeating these tactics he was enticed onwards again, until crossing an ice-couloir rendered dangerous through falling stones, I walked out on to the level glacier at the bottom to await him. Very slowly he crawled down, and when in the centre of the couloir, although I screamed to him to hurry, he was nearly hit by a great stone weighing half a hundredweight that had come from two or three thousand feet above. Although it only missed him by a few feet, he never changed his pace; and when at last he reached me, seated on a stone, he dropped full length on the ice, absolutely refusing to move, and groaning. He had eaten nothing for the last forty hours.

My position was becoming serious. I could not leave the Gurkha, Lubar was miles away down the glacier, and some of the rest of the party might be in the same condition as Ragobir. I could think of nothing except to smoke my pipe and wait for something to happen. Half an hour passed, then an hour; and then, far up on the summit of the Mazeno La a black dot appeared, and shortly afterwards two more. So I waited, and at last the whole party was reunited. Bruce managed to revive Ragobir, who had had over two hours' rest, and we all set off as fast as we could for the shepherds' huts at Lubar. As the sun was setting we arrived there, very weary, but buoyed up with the expectation of something to eat. I shall never forget the sight that greeted my eyes when Mummery and I, the last of the party, walked into the small enclosure of stones where the goats and sheep were collected.

Bruce was seated on the small wall in his shirt-sleeves, superintending the slaughter of one of the sheep. And, horrible to relate, in less than half an hour after we entered Lubar we were all ravenously devouring pieces of sheep's liver only half cooked on the ends of sticks.

The dirty, sour goats' milk, too, was delicious, and as far as I can recollect, each of us drank considerably over a gallon that evening, to wash down the fragments of toasted sheep and chappatties that we made from some flour that had providentially remained behind our caravan with a sick coolie. Very soon we got into a somewhat comatose condition, and there was some sort of arrangement made, that should any one wake in the night he should look after the fire. But next morning when I awoke the fire was out and I was covered with hoarfrost. We had all fallen asleep almost in the positions in which we sat in front of the fire.

I am afraid I must apologise for this second description of the delights of feeding after a prolonged fast. But few people have any conception of what it feels like to be really starving and worked till one longs to drop down anywhere—even on snow or ice. Hunger, exposure, and exhaustion are hard taskmasters, and the relief brought by rest, comfort, and plenty of food is a pleasure never to be forgotten. It is certainly one of the keenest enjoyments I have ever experienced.

Next morning we started for the Diamirai camp, taking with us the coolie and the precious flour. We preferred to strike out a new route, keeping higher up the mountain-side and more to the right. Before long we met some of our Kashmir servants who had come back from the Diamirai to look for us, and, as was their most excellent custom, brought with them as many edibles as they could. These of course were soon finished. We left them to return by the ordinary route to the camp, whilst we followed up the Butesharon glacier in a south-easterly direction, reaching at its head a col about 17,000 feet.

From this pass, on that perfectly clear afternoon,

an unsurpassed panorama was spread out before us. The Indus valley lay 14,000 feet beneath us. Beyond stretched that almost unknown land below Chilas. A hundred miles away were the snow peaks in the Swat country, marked on the map as 18,563 feet and 19,395 feet high, standing out distinct against the sky, whilst much further still, a little more to the right, rose a vast snow peak nearly flat topped, or at least a ridge of peaks, several thousand feet higher than any others. It was probably Tirach Mir above Chitral, 25,426 feet and 24,343 feet high.

From the summit of the Butesharon pass we descended almost straight to the camp, which had been pitched in the old spot, where we had been ten days before.

During the next two days, August 3 and 4, we stopped in camp, and on the 5th Bruce left us, going back to Abbottabad *via* the Mazeno La, the Kamri, and Kashmir. As we heard afterwards, it was anything but a pleasant journey, for, probably owing to the exposure during that night on Nanga Parbat, his complaint had been aggravated, and the glands of his neck and face had become so swollen, that when he was met by a friend on the Kamri he was unrecognisable, and for many months afterwards was unable to wear a collar.

The day that Bruce left, Mummery and I with

the Gurkhas started to explore the upper end of the Diamirai glacier. We camped at the head of the valley on the last grass on the northern side. Mummery and Ragobir started at midnight for the western face of Nanga Parbat. During the day they managed to reach the top of the second rib of rocks that lie directly under the summit, a height of about 17,000 to 18,000 feet. In the meantime I went to look at the Diama glacier between the Ganalo peak, 21,650 feet, and Nanga Parbat, taking with me Goman Singh and our Kashmir shikari. We climbed up the ridge that comes down from the Ganalo peak to about 17,000 feet, but unfortunately the day was cloudy, so I was unable satisfactorily to see the whole of the Diama valley, and ascertain what chances we should have if we were to attack Nanga Parbat from that side. However, on returning in the afternoon, I met Mummery on the glacier. He was delighted with his exploration, for there was, he said, magnificent climbing, and he had found a place on the top of the second rib of rock where a tent might be pitched.

From July 13, the day we left the Kishnganga valley, it had been gloriously fine; but next day, August 7, the weather broke with heavy rain. Of course all our energies now were concentrated on the ascent of Nanga Parbat. Mummery decided that we should push provisions and supplies up the route that he and Ragobir had prospected; and he was confident that once beyond the rock ribs and on the upper snow-fields with some provisions and a silk tent, it would be very hard luck indeed should we be driven back before we reached the summit.

During August 8 and 9, Mummery, Ragobir, Lor Khan (a Chilas shikari, who had come up from Gashut in the Bunar valley, and insisted on stopping with us), and I spent the time in carrying a waterproof bag of provisions and some odds and ends up the second rib of rock to a height of 17,150 feet. Here we left it in a safe place on the rocks. We also had considerable quantities of fuel taken up by coolies, to a camp 15,000 feet, at the bottom of the rocks under Nanga Parbat.

Mummery was not wrong when he said it was magnificent climbing. The only climbing in the Alps I can compare it to is that on the Chamounix Aiguilles. In many places it was similar to that on the west side of the Aiguille du Plan from the Pèlerin glacier.

Between the first and second ribs of rock the glacier was broken up into the wildest confusion, and it was only by passing a somewhat nasty couloir, down which occasional ice avalanches came, that the rocks of the second rib could be reached; thence to the top of the rib was difficult rock climbing over great slabs and towers of rock set at a very steep angle. I was extremely surprised that Lor Khan would go, but he did not seem in the least frightened, and with a little help from the rope climbed splendidly.

As we returned that night to our camp the rains descended, and we arrived wet through ; the weather was getting worse, and no serious attempt could be made for the present on Nanga Parbat.

CHAPTER VI

ASCENT OF THE DIAMIRAI PEAK

'Nothing that is mountainous is alien to us; we are addicted to all high places from Gaurisankar to Primrose Hill, wherever man has not forked out Nature. No doubt we find a particular fascination in the greatest and boldest inequalities of the earth's surface and the strange scenery of the ice and snow world; but we are attracted by any inequality, so long as it has not a railroad station or a restaurant on the top of it.'

DOUGLAS FRESHFIELD.

ABOUT this time we were beginning to run short of provisions, though a month earlier we had ordered all sorts of luxuries—jams, Kashmir wine, and so forth—from Srinagar, and had heard that they had been despatched to Bandipur, to be forwarded thence by the Government Commissariat Department. All inquiries were, however, fruitless, but Bruce had promised that should he, on his way down country to Abbottabad, discover their whereabouts he would hurry them on. Eventually he found them reposing at Bandipur, so he at once packed them on ponies and sent them to our camp in the Rupal nullah, knowing how the Commissariat Department had to strain every nerve to get the requisite grain supplies for the troops over the passes to Gilgit before the bad weather set in and blocked the Burzil, and that private baggage and supplies might wait indefinitely till such time as it pleased the Department to find ponies to convey them to their destination. Personally we did not wish to leave the Diamirai nullah, but at the same time it was absolutely necessary that somehow we should replenish our vanishing stock of food. Already two of our Kashmir servants had been sent down into the Bunar district to bring up whatever they were able to collect, but we could not depend on the Chilas nullahs to yield us all we might want. This question of provisioning our camp caused perpetual worry. Unless one has trustworthy servants, every ten days or so one of the party has to start off to the nearest village for supplies. This may take a week or more, and as the period during which the big mountains are in a condition to climb is at the best but very limited, much valuable time will be wasted.

Bruce told me that whilst he was with Sir W. M. Conway, in the Karakorams, all the catering was left to Rahim Ali, his servant. If every fortnight during their stay at the head of the Baltoro glacier they had been forced, as we were, personally to forage and seek for dilatory servants, the climbing on Pioneer peak would have progressed but slowly. A piece of advice which cannot be too strongly urged upon those who go to the Himalaya is to get good servants at any cost, not to grudge the time spent, for it will be regained afterwards a hundredfold. The cook or khansammah ought to be the chief servant in the camp. He ought to be responsible for everything: it is his business to provide food, and a good cook who feeds one well, and takes the responsibility of the endless small details of management and supply off one's shoulders is worth five times the wages which are usually given.

Accordingly, after some consultation, Hastings generously agreed to sacrifice himself and trudge back to our camp in the Rupal nullah and thence to Astor, not only with the hope of bringing back with him all the luxuries we had weeks before ordered from Srinagar, but also with the intention of procuring sheep, flour, rice, and tea from Astor. At the same time he hoped to shorten to a great extent the journey to the Mazeno by making a new and direct pass over into the Lubar nullah immediately south of our camp. In the meantime Mummery and I were to stay behind in the

Diamirai nullah and push provisions up the face of Nanga Parbat as fast as we could.

Just south of our camp rose a snow peak, about 19,000 feet, which we have called the Diamirai peak. On July 24, in crossing the pass from the Diamirai over to the Lubar glacier, we had left it on our right. It is not on the main ridge of Nanga Parbat, but on a side spur running to the westward. Camped as we were at its very foot, and looking on it as but a single day's climb, we determined to try to ascend it, whilst we waited for the snow to clear off the rocks on Nanga Parbat. By this time we had learned that the ascent of any peak 20,000 feet high was a laborious undertaking. At first we had talked about the 'twenty thousanders' somewhat contemptuously, and not without reason, for our hopes were fixed on Nanga Parbat, 26,629 feet; surely if a mountain of that height were possible, those whose summits were 7000 feet lower ought to be simplicity itself. In fact, we imagined that, as far as difficulty was concerned, they should stand somewhat in the same proportion to each other as an ascent of Mont Blanc to a climb up the Brévent from Chamounix during the springtime before all the snow has melted.

Unfortunately they were not quite so easy as

The Diamirai Peak from the Red Pass

we should have liked; not only did they involve an ascent from the camp of 7000 to 8000 feet, but also a considerable amount of the climbing under a pressure of about half an atmosphere. Then the interminable ice slopes, which in the Nanga Parbat district are very much more common than in the Alps, meant many hours of step-cutting, and the softened state of the snow directly after the sun had shone on it added considerably to our labour. Besides these drawbacks, which render the ascent of a mountain 20,000 feet high not altogether easy, the utter confusion and wearisome monotony of the stony and rugged hill-sides between the valley and the snow-line must not be forgotten.

On August the 11th, we all started early in the morning by lantern light, taking with us Ragobir and Lor Khan (as well as Goman Singh and two coolies who were to accompany Hastings as far as Astor). We first climbed up a small moraine coming steeply down the side of the main valley almost to our camp from the glacier on the north-west side of the Diamirai peak, and in about an hour and a half came to the glacier itself. Here Hastings parted company with us, and, crossing a pass (which he has named Goman Singh pass), to the westward of the Diamirai peak, got safely over down to the Lubar glacier, whence by way of the Mazeno pass he came to our camp in the Rupal nullah. Mummery and I, accompanied by Ragobir and Lor Khan, turning slightly to the left, made for a gully leading higher up to a snow ridge which ran upwards nearly to the summit of the peak. At the foot of the gully we were confronted by a small bergschrund. This we easily turned, and began scrambling up the rocks on our left hand.

Gradually the grey dawn melted into a Himalayan sunrise. Far away over the lower ridges we could see—

> 'The ever-silent spaces of the east
> Far folded mists, and gleaming halls of morn.'

Above there was very little colour, pale greens verging into oranges and yellows, whilst below, in the shadows of the valleys, cold, dark steel blues, clear and deep, were the predominating shades. For a long while we watched the orange sunlight, catching first one part of Nanga Parbat and then another, as slowly the patches widened and spread creeping always down the mountain-side. Away to the north, on the opposite side of the Diamirai nullah, two minor rock peaks on the ridge were tipped with the rays of the morning sun. At the height we had already gained there was visible over the intervening ridge all the

VIEW OF THE DIAMIRAI PE

The dotted lines show our various routes.

ROM THE RED PASS.

country above Gor on the further side of the Indus, while to the south of Gilgit stretched away mile after mile of mountain ranges. But by far the most striking sight was the enormous snow range beyond Gilgit and Yasin, the extreme western end of the Mustagh or Karakoram range. Rakipushi we could not see; it was just cut off by the western spur of the Ganalo peak, but from a point just west of the Kilik pass almost to the mountains above Chitral, snow summit after snow summit rose up into the heavens clear cut and distinct in the wonderfully translucent air.

With this marvellous view nothing interfered, as the average height of the peaks on this mighty barrier which divides English from Russian territory cannot be much less than 23,000 feet, and that of the hills which lay between us and these peaks was not more than 16,000 feet. High above the great snow range on the horizon, a long-drawn cloud floated like a grey bar of silver, but it did not prevent the rays of the rising sun from covering with their golden light the whole of the distant and lonely snow world, as yet untrodden by the foot of man. As usual, a perfect stillness and calm in the morning air seemed to herald a fine day, but already we had learned to mistrust these signs:—

'Full many a glorious morning have I seene,
Flatter the mountaine tops with soveraine eie,

Anon permit the basest cloudes to ride
With ougly rack on his celestiall face.'

Few days were there during our stay in the Nanga Parbat region that were clear after 10 A.M., and this morning was no exception.

The sun had risen above Nanga Parbat, and we knew well how soon the snow would soften under its powerful rays—half an hour usually sufficing under these conditions to thaw through the frozen outer crust. New snow, too, had fallen in considerable quantities, so we did not want to waste any of the valuable early hours on the lower slopes. Fortunately about this time the morning mists began to gather as usual, and not only prevented the snow from melting, but protected us from the fearful glare which would have been our fate on a perfectly cloudless day. Very narrow and steep was the snow ridge which stretched up the mountain-side above us, but we knew, although we could not see from where we were, that it led almost to the summit. The average angle of the arête was a little over 40 degrees. At first Mummery was easily able to nick out steps with the axe, but soon the crust began to give way here and there, leaving us to struggle often knee-deep. On our right the angle was not very steep, but on the left of the ridge was a most forbidding ice slope. Every now and then we would make rapid progress, finding a thinner coating of snow upon the ice, with but one or two small crevasses to be crossed. Away on our left was an excellent rock ridge, but we could not reach it without cutting across the steep ice-slope. However, our arête, some distance further up, seemed to join the rock ridge, so we pushed on quickly, in the hope that above we should be rewarded by finding easy rocks to climb. Before we reached this point a difficult and steep piece on the arête had to be surmounted. If we could have traversed off to the right it would have been easier, but the snow was in a most unstable condition; small zigzags to the right and then back again on to the ridge were resorted to, and ultimately we succeeded in getting up this somewhat nasty place. Rapid progress was then made, but we found, much to our disappointment, that the rock ridge ended where it joined the arête, and our hopes of an easy rock climb vanished.

Finally we arrived just under the first summit of our mountain. Here the same difficulty we had experienced down below again presented itself, but in a worse form. The arête was much steeper, sloping probably at an angle of about 55 to 60 degrees. Mummery tried the same tactics as before, but soon had to confess that he dared not trust the snow any further, for it was thoroughly sodden upon the surface of the ice, and we might bring the whole face off at any moment. On the arête itself the snow, where it had drifted and been frozen, lay curiously deep, so that even at the thinnest point it did not allow of steps being cut in the ice below. Our only chance, therefore, was to try the ice slope on the left of the arête. Mummery led, cutting the steps diagonally across the slope, where a thin coating of snow lay some two or three inches deep over the hard ice underneath. As he moved slowly upwards, I came next on the rope, and, to keep my hands employed, passed the time in cutting the steps deeper into the ice.

The position was a sensational one—we were crossing the steepest ice slope of any great size I had ever been on; below us it shot straight down some 2000 feet without a break, till the angle became less in a small snow basin. The next objects that met the eye were the stone slopes far below in the valley, and unconsciously I began to picture to myself the duration and the result of an involuntary glissade on such a mountain-side.

Lor Khan, who came behind me on the rope, seemed to be enjoying himself immensely; of course he had never been in such a position before, but these Chilas tribesmen are famous fellows. What Swiss peasant, whilst making his first trial of the big snow peaks and the ice, would have dared to follow in such a place, and that, too, with only skins soaked through by the melting snow wrapped round his feet? Lor Khan never hesitated for a moment; when I turned and pointed downwards he only grinned, and looked as if he were in the habit of walking on ice slopes every day of his life. We were soon all in a line across this ice face, and whilst I was cutting one of Mummery's steps deeper to make it safer for our Chilas shikari, I noticed that the rope was hanging down in a great loop between Lor Khan and myself. At once I cried out to him not to move again till it was absolutely tight between us, and always to keep it so for the future. In the East we found that people were accustomed to obey instantly without asking questions. What the sahib said was law, at least so long as the sahib was there himself to enforce obedience. Consequently as I moved onward the rope soon became taut, and fortunately remained in that condition. Shortly after this Mummery turned upwards and slightly to his right, cutting nearly straight up the face, owing to some bad snow which barred our way. Just as I began the ascent of this staircase I heard a startled exclamation below. Instinctively I struck the pick of my axe deep into the ice, and at the same moment the whole of the weight of the unfortunate Lor Khan came on Ragobir and on me with the full force of a drop of some five to six feet. He had slipped out of one of the steps, and hung with his face to the glistening ice, whilst under him the thin coating of snow peeled off the face of the slope in great and ever-widening masses, gathering in volume as it plunged headlong down the mountain-side, finally to disappear over the cliffs thousands of feet below. For the time being I was fascinated by the descending avalanche, my whole mind being occupied with but this one thought, that if Lor Khan began to struggle and jerk at the rope I should without a doubt be pulled out of my steps. My fears proved groundless. Although Lor Khan had lost his footing he never lost either his head or his axe, and was just able to reach with his hand one of the steps out of which he had fallen. After Mummery had made himself quite firm above me I found myself, with the help of Ragobir, who was last on the rope, just able to haul up our Chilas shikari to a step which he had manfully cut for himself. It was, however, a very unpleasant experience; if the fall had been ten feet instead of six, I should never have been able to have borne the strain, and Lor Khan would have fallen considerably more than that if he had not been opportunely warned that he must keep the rope tight between himself and me.

Half an hour later we got off our ice slope and stepped almost on to the first summit. All our difficulties were over. After ploughing through some soft snow, at about half-past eleven o'clock we were seated on the true top of our peak, the height of which by the barometer turned out to be 19,000 feet.

We had climbed between 6000 and 7000 feet, and Mummery had led the whole way. The last 3000 feet had been very severe, for at first most of the steps had to be laboriously broken, and later we had to win our way by the use of the axe. But Mummery was perfectly fresh and could have gone on for hours, the diminished pressure (fifteen inches of mercury) having apparently no effect on him; neither was Ragobir any the worse for his climb; Lor Khan and I had slight headaches, but otherwise were quite fit for more. As we sat on the top enveloped in mist, Mummery and I debated afresh the old question, How should we feel if we ever ascended to 26,000 feet? Mummery reasoned that it would chiefly depend on our state of training at the time. Had I not been dreadfully ill at 18,000 feet crossing the Mazeno La, whilst here we were all right at 19,000 feet? Had we not ascended our last 3000 feet with hardly a rest and at exactly the same pace as if we had been climbing in the Alps? As it always takes two to argue, I perforce had to try my best as the opposition. At once I discovered that my headache was by no means a negligible quantity, and was therefore an excellent test for abnormal altitudes. Probably also mountain-sickness was a disease which lurked in the higher mountains and was ready at any moment to rush on and seize its prey. Luckily for us the particular bacillus was not just then in the surrounding atmosphere, consequently we had not been inoculated, yet perhaps should we on some future occasion go to 21,000 to 22,000 feet, we might be suddenly overwhelmed. Then I quoted an article I had read somewhere about paralysis and derangement of nerve-centres in the spinal column being the fate of all who insist on energetic action when the barometer stands at thirteen inches. It was no good, Mummery only laughed at me; and at this moment the mist clearing for a short space to the southward, we were soon far more interested with the view of the Thosho and Rupal peaks. The summit we were on fell away on the south directly under our feet in a series of rock precipices. We started on our homeward journey at about one o'clock without catching a single glimpse of Nanga Parbat. The descent of the steep ice slopes of our upward route was far too dangerous to attempt, so we decided on a rock ridge to the westward which we hoped would lead us down on the pass that Hastings had crossed earlier in the day.

Ragobir was sent to the front. He led us down the most precipitous places with tremendous rapidity and immense enjoyment. It was all 'good' according to him, and his cheery face down below made me feel that there could be no difficulty, till I found myself hanging down a slab of rock with but the barest of handholds, or came to a bulging mass of ice overhanging a steep gully, which insisted on protruding into the middle of my stomach, with direful result to my state of equilibrium.

At one place where the ridge was a narrow knife edge, with precipices on both sides, we had a splendid piece of climbing. A sharp descent of about a hundred feet occurred on the arête which seemed at first sight impossible. Ragobir tried first on the right hand, but, owing to the smoothness of the rock slabs and the absence of all handholds, was unable to get down further than twenty feet or so. Whilst I was dangling the Gurkha on the end of the rope, Mummery discovered what he considered to be a possible solution of the difficulty. Ragobir was to climb about twenty-five feet down a small open chimney on the perpendicular south face of the ridge; he then would be on the top of a narrow flake of rock which was laid against the mountain-side in the same manner as those on the traverse of the Aiguille de Grépon. We could easily hold him from above whilst he edged sideways along this narrow way. After a short time he called out that it was all right, and I let down Lor Khan next. When I myself got on to the traverse I was very much impressed, not that it was very difficult, thanks to the splendid handholds, but the face was so perpendicular that without them one could hardly have stood on the narrow top of the slab without falling outwards. A loose stone when thrown out about twenty feet pitched on some snow at least five hundred feet below.

I found Ragobir and Lor Khan on a small niche on the ridge which divided the arête into two and at the top of an incipient ice gully. With considerable difficulty I managed to squeeze on to the small platform of rock and direct operations. Ragobir cut his way down to the next place where he could rest; and, after carefully hitching the rope as safely as I could, Mummery was called on to follow. It was just the kind of place he enjoyed, but it needed some one with iron nerves to descend the somewhat difficult chimney and then edge along the traverse without a steadying-rope from above. After the descent of the ice gully the climbing proved much easier. Rapid progress was made in spite of an uncertainty as to where we were going, for everything was hidden by the afternoon mists. Our route kept slowly bending away to the south-west, and as Hastings's pass lay directly to the west, we hoped that another bend to the north-west would put us straight again.

We could not leave the ridge and traverse to our right, so perforce had to keep on descending, and when at last the mists did rise for a short time, we found our fears amply confirmed. The pass lay about a thousand feet above on our right, and, what was still more exasperating, the shortest route to it necessitated a still further descent of at least five hundred feet, followed by a traverse underneath the overhanging end of a glacier. An extra fifteen hundred feet of climbing up the unstable, interminable, and heart-breaking debris, which is so common on the south faces of the Himalaya, and that, too, late in the afternoon, was trying even to the best of tempers. I used quite unpublishable language, and even the imperturbable Mummery was moved to express his feelings in much more forcible language than was customary. There are occasions when language fails, and even the pen of Rudyard Kipling is unequal to depict the situation literally, though he does his best. There rises before me his description of that scene in the railway works at Jamalpur, where an apprentice is addressing, 'half in expostulation and half in despair, a very much disorganised engine which is sadly in need of repair.' Kipling gives us the gist of his language, but owns that after all the youth put it 'more crisply—very much more crisply.'

We reached the top at last, but even then we had to traverse to the westward half a mile before beginning the descent. Once started we went at racing speed, sometimes getting a long glissade down soft snow, sometimes a run down small stone debris; it was rather hard on poor Lor Khan, who was not shod for this kind of work, and was soon left far behind.

But it was getting late, and we wished to reach the camp before dark. Just as the sun was setting over the far-away hills in the wild, unknown Tangir, and shining through a thin veil of an evening shower, the tents under the Diamirai moraine were sighted; and during the after-dinner smoke opposite a roaring fire of pine logs we went over our day's adventures, and both agreed that we had enjoyed ourselves hugely: and so to bed.

CHAPTER VII

ATTEMPT TO ASCEND NANGA PARBAT

'An ancient peak, in that most lonely land,
Snow-draped and desolate, where the white-fleec'd clouds
Like lagging sheep are wandering all astray,
Till the shrill whistling wind, their shepherd rude,
Drives them before him at the early dawn
To feed upon the barren mountain tops.
Far from the stately pines, whose branches woo
The vagrant breeze with murmuring melody,
Far from the yellow cornlands, far from streams
And dewy lawns soft cradled deep below,
Naked it stands. The cold wind's goblin prate,
Of weird lost legends born in days of old,
Echoes all night amongst its pinnacles;
Whilst higher more remote a storm-swept dome
Mocks the pale moon: there nothing living reigns
Save one old spirit of a forgotten God.'

FRAGMENT.

A WEEK before this, on the same day that Bruce had left us, our cook and our head shikari, together with some coolies, had been sent to fetch up from the Bunar valley any provisions they could find. We knew that if they had travelled with ordinary speed, five days was ample for the whole journey, and they were therefore two days overdue. Moreover, in our camp provisions for

On Nanga Parbat, from Upper Camp

only one day remained. Our position was annoying. Of course, as the weather had turned fine again we wished to carry more necessaries up to the camp at the head of the Diamirai glacier, just under Nanga Parbat; but even where we were at the base camp, it was two days' hard travelling from the nearest village and food. This position of affairs produced a long discussion, and finally we agreed that we ourselves must go down to Bunar after the dilatory servants. It was most provoking, but there was no help for it. Leaving the camp in charge of the goat-herd from the Lubar nullah, and our water-carrier or bhisti, Mummery and I started off with Lor Khan and some servants for Bunar. The further we went the worse the path became, but by skirting upwards along the hill-side, on the left of the valley, we soon left the Diamirai glacier far below us. About this point we met our head shikari, who had come on in front of the remainder of the party from Bunar—at least he said so, but we could get very little accurate information out of him. In fact, as we afterwards discovered, he had stopped at the first village he had come to, and remained there doing nothing, or at least nothing connected with getting us provisions, which work he left to the cook. After enjoying himself for three days in this manner, thinking it was time to return, and collecting what he could, namely some grapes and apples, he came back to us with them as a peace-offering. Whilst he had been away, however, unfortunately for him, our other servants had explained several curious things which we at the time did not understand. These explanations left in our minds no doubt that this wretched Kashmir shikari had not only been robbing us, but also all the coolies as well. We in our ignorance thought that if the coolies were paid with our own hands, the money at least would be safe. In the East this is by no means the case, for the moment we were out of sight, this wily old ruffian would return to the coolies, telling them that they had been overpaid, and that the Sahibs commanded them instantly to give back half of the money. Our coolies were mostly Baltis from the Astor district. These poor Baltis have been a downtrodden race for centuries, harried by their more warlike and courageous neighbours — the Chilasis and the robbers of Gilgit and Hunza. So the shikari has no difficulty in making them yield to his extortion.

Mummery for some time listened to his obvious lying, but soon lost his temper. A coolie anxious to go to his home in the Rupal nullah here served our purpose. The shikari was told to return to the Rupal nullah with him, and at the same time we gave him a letter to Hastings. In that letter, which he could not read, we explained the situation, and instructed Hastings to pay the shikari off and send him about his business.

The route we were following soon turned away to the left, leaving the Diamirai nullah on the right. It was afterwards that we found out the reason for this. It seems to be impossible to descend or ascend this portion of the Diamirai nullah direct. The valley narrows in below the bottom of the glacier, and finally becomes a deep gorge with cliffs thousands of feet high on either side. Our change in direction soon showed us that we should have to cross the tributary Lubar nullah. This meant that we had to climb down a very steep rocky face of about 3000 feet. At about four in the afternoon we arrived at the bottom, finding an impassable glacier torrent thundering over great boulders and swollen by the melted snows of the morning. Walls of rock barred our way either up or down the stream, but Lor Khan said we were at the ford. In vain we tried to place pine trunks across—they were swept away one by one. It was a fine sight to see Lor Khan, stripped to the waist, struggling in the icy water with the great pine stems, a magnificent specimen of fearlessness, muscle, and activity. Fortunately we had insisted on roping him, for once he was carried off his feet and had to be brought back to land half drowned but laughing. It soon became perfectly evident that we could not cross till early next morning, when the frost on the glaciers above would have frozen up the sources of this turbulent stream. As we were wondering where we could possibly find room to lie down for the night, high above us on the opposite bank a stone came bounding down a precipitous gully. Who had started it? Some goat or other wild animal; or was it our cook returning with provisions? Shouting was useless, for the roar of the torrent drowned every noise. Five minutes passed, then ten, finally a quarter of an hour, but we were not destined to be disappointed; at last, more than five hundred feet up the gully opposite, we saw our cook with all the coolies.

After they had descended, a rope was thrown across to them, and we succeeded by its aid in hauling a slippery pine trunk into position behind two large stones. Over this we crossed and camped on a narrow spit of level ground underneath the perpendicular walls of rock: chickens, sugar, eggs, three maunds of flour, and four sheep were amongst the spoils brought up by our cook from Bunar.

That evening we ate our meal by the ruddy light of a great camp fire, with the roar of the torrent making it almost impossible to hear our voices, and underneath some gnarled and stunted pines, whose roots were firmly imbedded in the great fissures that ran up the perpendicular rock face. As the question of provisions had been settled for some time, we returned much relieved in our minds to the Diamirai nullah.

The next day, August 14th, it again rained hard nearly all day. At 2 A.M. on the 15th we started once more for the upper camp. We took with us Ragobir, Lor Khan, and a Chilasi coolie, whom I had called Richard the Third, from his likeness to the usual portraits of that monarch. More firewood and provisions and a silk tent were taken up to this camp at the head of the glacier. Two rucksacks had already been left high up on the rocks on the 9th. It was now Mummery's intention to take some more odds and ends up to where they were, and if possible push on with about a third of the provisions to about 20,000 feet, and leave them there for the final attempt. This necessitated sleeping on the top of the second rib of rocks. By the time I had arrived at the upper camp underneath Nanga Parbat I began to develop a headache, and, being otherwise ill as well, I had reluctantly to give up any idea of climbing further. Mummery, Ragobir, and Lor Khan went on, whilst I spent most of the morning watching them climb like flies up the almost perpendicular rib of rocks above me.

But I had to get home that night, and also get the coolie home as well. This was no easy matter, for there were some steep ice slopes, with steps cut in them, and crevasses at the bottom, which so frightened poor Richard the Third, that for a long time I could not induce him even to try. In fact, ultimately I had to threaten him violently with my ice-axe. Whether he thought that it was a choice of death by cold steel above, or cold ice below in the crevasse, I don't know, but he chose the latter, and was much surprised to find that he was not going to be sacrificed after all. Then, before we got home it began to rain heavily, the mists came down, everything becoming dull and dreary, the wind sighed sorrowfully up and down the valley, and I was sorry for Mummery on the inhospitable slopes of the great mountain. Mummery spent the night on the top of the second rib of rocks, and next day he climbed about a thousand feet up the third rib, where he left a rucksack with food. The climb was carried out almost entirely in mist; in fact, in the afternoon down at the camp the mist and rain made things thoroughly uncomfortable. I was beginning

Nanga Parbat from the Diamirai Glacier

to get anxious about Mummery, for he did not come back by sunset, and the night promised to be one of drenching rain. But later, in the dark, he marched back into camp, entirely wet through, but far more cheerful than the circumstances warranted, and very pleased with the climbing. His account of the ice world on Nanga Parbat was wonderful. Nowhere in the Caucasus had he seen anything to compare with it. Avalanches had fallen down thousands of feet, set at an angle of over 60 degrees, that would have almost swept away towns. The crevasses were enormous, and the rock-climbing, although difficult, was set at such a steep angle that no time would be lost in making height towards the upper glacier underneath the final peak. If only the weather would clear, Mummery was sure that we could get on to this upper glacier. But the weather sulked and was against us, it rained nearly all the next day, finishing up with a tremendous thunderstorm. In hope that fine weather would now set in, we turned into our tents for the night. About midnight, gusts of cold wind began to moan amongst the stunted pines that surrounded our tents; then, gathering in force, this demon of the mountains howled round our tents, and snow came down in driven sheets. The anger of the spirits that inhabited the mountains had been roused, we were being informed of what awaited us, should we persist in our impious endeavours to penetrate into the sanctuaries above.

Many times in the pitch darkness of the night I thought the small Mummery tent I was in would be simply torn in pieces, but towards daylight the hurricane gradually died away, and by nine o'clock the sun came out. The scene, when I emerged from the tent, I shall never forget. Bright sunshine and dazzling white snow—but where were all the groves of rhododendron bushes, from four to five feet high, that yesterday had surrounded our camp? Loaded with the snow, they had been beaten flat, and lay there plastered and stuck tight to the ground, by the ice and snow of the blizzard of the night before.

But under the double action of the sun's heat and the rapid evaporation that takes place when the barometer stands only at about sixteen inches, the snow, which was over six inches deep, soon melted, and by the afternoon had all disappeared from around our camp. On the morrow a cloudless sky and a northerly wind changed the whole aspect of affairs.

We had a long consultation, Mummery arguing that we ought to start for Nanga Parbat at once, and make an attempt to reach the summit. His

NANGA PARBAT FROM THE DIAMIRAI GLACIER.

A—Upper Camp at the base of Nanga Parbat.
B—First rib of rocks.
C—Second rib of rocks.
D—Sleeping-place on the top of the second rib of rocks.
E—Third rib of rocks.
F—Mr. A. F. Mummery's highest point (over 20,000 feet).
G—The foot of the Diama Glacier.
H—The Diamirai Glacier.

The dotted line shows route taken.

only fear was that Hastings would feel that we were not treating him fairly by starting before he had returned from Astor and could join us in the climb. But the weather had been changeable, and the Chilas coolies with us were predicting that when the next snowstorm came, it would be worse than the last, and the snow would not clear away so quickly. There seemed great probability in their predictions. At any rate, with the cold north wind the good weather would last, but we ought to make use of that good weather at once.

So, hoping that Hastings would forgive us, we started on the final attempt to reach the summit of Nanga Parbat.

Our position was as follows:—We had plenty of provisions and firewood at the camp at the head of the glacier, a tent and more provisions with some spirits and a boiling tin on the top of the second ridge of rocks, and a last rucksack with more edibles half way up the third rib of rock.

On the evening of the 18th, Mummery, Ragobir, and I slept at the camp at the head of the glacier (15,000 feet), but next morning they went on alone, for the coarse food of the previous three weeks had not agreed with me: flour that is largely composed of grindstone is apt to upset one's digestion. Again I sat for a whole morning watching them crawl slowly up that second rib of rock. Once they were hidden from my sight in a huge cloud of snow dust, the fringe of one of those tremendous avalanches that I have only seen in the Himalaya. At last, becoming too small to follow with the eye, they disappeared from my sight.

That night I was again back in the base camp. There I found a note from Hastings that had been sent on ahead from the Lubar nullah with the goat-herd and a coolie; and the next day Hastings himself arrived with large quantities of provisions. He had been as far as Astor, and said that without the invaluable help of Goman Singh he would never have got the coolies back over the Mazeno La.

Late that night Mummery and Ragobir came into camp. They had passed the second night on the summit of the second rib of rocks. Next morning, starting before daylight, they had pushed on up the final rib towards the upper snow-field. The climbing, Mummery admitted, was excessively difficult, but the higher he went the easier it became. Finally, at a height of over 20,000 feet, for he could see over the Nanga Parbat col on his right, Ragobir turned ill: it was therefore folly to attempt to spend another night on the mountain at that height. Reluctantly he had to return; and his disappointment was great, for, as he said, most of the difficulties had been overcome below the upper snow-field, and he was confident that had he reached these upper snows and been able to spend another night on the mountain, he might have reached the summit on the following day.

Thus ended the only attempt Mummery made to reach the summit of Nanga Parbat.

I shall always look upon it as one of his finest climbs. Part of it I know from personal experience, and from Mummery's description of the upper half, there must have been some magnificent climbing, surrounded by an ice world such as can be seen nowhere except on peaks with at least 15,000 feet of snow on them. But it was on too large a scale for ordinary mortals, and the difficulties began just above the camp, at the head of the glacier, 12,000 feet below the summit of the mountain. Although the last 6000 feet of the mountain does not look as if it would present much difficulty or danger, yet above 20,000 feet one would necessarily make height very slowly, and much step-cutting would be almost impossible at that height.

The following two days were spent in discussing what we should do next; for Mummery had very sorrowfully come to the conclusion that his route up Nanga Parbat from the Diamirai glacier must be abandoned.

Ultimately it was agreed that, owing to all the recent snowfalls, a purely snow route was the only one that would give any chance of success. Our last chance lay in finding such a route; in the Rakiot nullah, there perhaps Nanga Parbat might be less precipitous. So thither we determined to go.

When Mummery and Ragobir had come down from the mountain, they did not bring with them the rucksacks from the top of the second rib of rocks. These were too valuable to leave behind. Mummery, disliking the interminable scrambling over loose stones which he would have to endure should he come with the coolies, suggested that the two Gurkhas should be sent early on the 23rd up the glacier to fetch the rucksacks down to the camp at the head of the Diamirai glacier. Here later in the day Mummery should join them, and from this point he could go up the Diama glacier which lay between Nanga Parbat and the Ganalo peak, 21,650 feet high. A snow pass (Diama pass) would then separate them from the Rakiot nullah. He left us on the 23rd, and took with him Lor Khan, and Rosamir, our head coolie, to carry some extra provisions up to the higher camp. That evening they were joined by Ragobir and Goman Singh, who had successfully brought down the rucksacks.

VIEW OF DIAMA GLACIER FROM SLOPES OF DIAMIRAI PEAK.

The arrow shows the route taken by Mr. A. F. Mummery on 24th August.

Next morning, the 24th August, Lor Khan and Rosamir, having seen them start off up the Diama valley to the east, returned down the Diamirai valley and joined us later. Mummery, Ragobir, and Goman Singh were never seen again.

CHAPTER VIII

THE INDUS VALLEY AND THIRD JOURNEY TO DIAMIRAI NULLAH

> 'For some . . .
> Have drunk their Cup a Round or two before,
> And one by one crept silently to rest.'
>
> *Rubáiyát of* OMAR KHAYYÁM.

OUR route with the coolies was to skirt along the lower slopes of Nanga Parbat as near the snow line as possible. This would lead us first into the Ganalo nullah, and thence to the Rakiot nullah. There we had arranged to meet Mummery by the side of the glacier. Having crossed the Diamirai glacier, we went straight up the opposite side of the valley for a pass on the ridge south-east of a pointed rock peak at the head of the Gonar nullah. This peak we have named the Gonar peak, and the pass the Red pass (about 16,000 feet). From this pass a superb view of the head of the Diamirai nullah was obtained, whilst to the south and south-west a beautifully shaped snow mountain, beyond the Lubar glacier, probably the Thosho peak, shone in the sunlight over the Goman

Singh pass. To the east we saw for the first time the great Chongra peaks on the north-east of Nanga Parbat. On the north side of our pass snow slopes stretched down some hundreds of feet to a small glacier. Some of the coolies tried an impromptu glissade here, and seemed rather pleased at the result; but it was a dangerous experiment, for various rocks and stones awaited their arrival at the bottom. At last in the dark after much trouble we managed to get down far enough to collect wood for our camp fires, and put up our tent by the side of a small stream.

Next day it was found necessary to climb up again at least 1000 feet before descending about 2500 feet on to the snout of the Ganalo glacier. This we crossed on the ice. On the far bank most luxuriant vegetation covered the hill-side, and for a long time we climbed rapidly upwards through woods of pines, birches, and other trees till the rhododendrons were reached late in the afternoon. Still we pushed on, hoping to get over into the Rakiot nullah, for perhaps Mummery would be there awaiting tents and food. But the coolies were dead beat; therefore, when we were still more than 1000 feet below the col, we were forced to camp beyond the limit of the brushwood in an open grass valley.

Next day we went over the pass, about 16,500 feet, into the Rakiot nullah. From the summit a splendid view of the Rakiot glacier and the northern side of Nanga Parbat could be seen. Never have I seen a glacier that presented such a sea of stormy ruin; the waste of frozen billows stretched ever upwards towards the ice-slopes that guarded the topmost towers of the great mountain. Thunder and rain welcomed us, and amidst dripping trees and cold mist our camp was pitched on the true left bank of the glacier. From the top of the last pass we had come over we could see the great face down which Mummery and the Gurkhas would have had to come had they reached the Diama pass. It seemed to us quite hopeless. I spent about half an hour looking through a powerful telescope for any traces of steps cut down the only ridge that looked at all feasible. I could see none. Hastings and I were therefore of the opinion that Mummery had turned back. This he had told us he intended to do should he find the pass either dangerous or very difficult, for, as he pointed out, he was not going to risk anything on an ordinary pass. Moreover, he had expressly taken sufficient food with him, leaving it at the upper camp, so that should he have to return and follow our footsteps he would

The Diama Pass from the Rakiot Nullah

have enough to last him for three days. In the Rakiot nullah we could find no traces of him. Lor Khan and Rosamir were at once sent back into the Ganalo nullah to meet Mummery with extra food, Hastings and I in the meantime exploring some distance up the valley. The day was more or less wet, with the mists lying low down on the mountains. It cleared, however, in the evening. The next two days were also wet and disagreeable. We were beginning to get anxious, and when on the 29th Lor Khan and the coolie returned, having seen nothing of Mummery, something had to be done.

We imagined that when the pass had proved to be too difficult, Mummery had turned back to the high camp where the food had been left. From there he would follow our route, but as the weather had been wretched, with mist lying over all the hills, perhaps he had missed his way. Or perhaps he might have sprained an ankle and be still in the Diamirai nullah. It was therefore agreed that Hastings should return towards the Diamirai nullah, and as my time was nearly at an end, if I wished to get back to England by the end of September, I should make my way to Astor as quickly as I could. Once there, I could wait a few days, and Hastings promised that as soon as possible he would send a coolie down to the nearest spot on the Gilgit-Chilas road, where there was a telegraph-station, and telegraph the news to me at Astor.

Thus we parted company, Hastings returning along our old route to the Diamirai, whilst I with a coolie and the cook set off for Astor.

About a mile down the valley we were met by some of the wild folk from Gor, a village on the opposite side of the Indus. These inhabitants of Gor have a somewhat evil reputation. Not many years before, an officer out shooting in one of their nullahs was nearly murdered. They did succeed in killing his shikari who was with him, but he himself escaped owing to the lucky appearance of some soldiers from Gilgit who were going down the valley of the Indus towards Chilas. Bruce also had some experience of these turbulent tribesmen when stopping at Darang, on the banks of the Indus below Gor; for whilst partridge-shooting in the hill-sides the beaters had to be armed with rifles, and played the double *rôle* of protecting Bruce and driving the game. The Gor shepherds that I met were, I believe, the only ones on the south side of the Indus. Owing to the rich pasturage in the Rakiot nullah, they kept sheep and goats there. I must say they treated me very well, and two of them

The Chongra Peaks from the Red Pass.

accompanied me for a couple of days, carrying the rucksacks and showing us the way.

The first night we slept in an old and disused shepherd's encampment high up, just at the limits of the pines. Next day we had to descend by most precipitous slopes to the bottom of the Buldar nullah. Our second night was spent high up on the eastern slopes of the nullah and short of the pass which was called the Liskom pass by the natives.

On the next day we crossed this pass (about 16,000 feet). The view of the Chongra peaks from here is most striking, backed as it is by the great upper snow-field of the Rakiot glacier and Nanga Parbat behind. Just across the Astor valley to the east rises the Dichil peak, a terrific, double-headed rock pinnacle that is certainly over 20,000 feet high.

These obliging Gor shepherds had accompanied us thus far, but no amount of persuasion could induce them to go one step further. At last, becoming frightened, they put the bags down on the snow and fled down the hill-side back to the Buldar nullah, and I was unable to give them anything for all their kindness. That afternoon, 1st September, I reached Dashkin on the Gilgit road, and was back again in civilised country. From there I made my way to Astor.

It was on the 5th of September that I received a telegram from Hastings. He had returned to the Diamirai nullah without finding Mummery. The camp there was just as we had left it. Next day, 1st September, he made his way up the glacier to the high camp under Nanga Parbat with Rosamir and Lor Khan; there he found the extra provisions and some other things exactly as they had been placed by Mummery on the morning of the 24th There was only one conclusion to draw—Mummery, Ragobir, and Goman Singh had been killed somewhere up the glacier that lies between the Ganalo peak and Nanga Parbat. For there was absolutely no way out, except the way they had gone in. The Diama pass over to the Rakiot nullah we knew to be impossible on the eastern face, on the south lay Nanga Parbat, whilst on the north was the Ganalo peak, 21,500 feet high. If, therefore, they never returned for the provisions, some catastrophe must have overtaken them during their attempt to climb over the pass.

From what I have seen of the valley, an avalanche falling from the north face of Nanga Parbat seems the most probable explanation; but in that vast ice world the hidden dangers are so many that any suggestion must necessarily be the merest guessing, and what happened we shall never know.

For Hastings to attempt to explore this glacier alone would have been a most hazardous and hopeless task. He had no one with him on whom he could rely, and the area to be explored was also far too large. His only alternative therefore was to go at once with the greatest speed possible to the nearest post where he knew an Englishman was, namely at Chilas. This he did, but it was not till the 5th of September that he reached Jiliper on the Indus and was able to telegraph to me at Astor.

In the meantime the villagers in the Bunar nullah had been ordered by the officer in command at Chilas to explore all the valleys round the Diamirai, and on the receipt of the telegram at Astor, Captain Stewart, the head political officer of the Gilgit district, sent word to the people in the Rupal nullah to do the same as far as the Mazeno La. I felt, however, that there was no help and no hope. Out of that valley up which Mummery had gone there was but one way: that was the one by which he had entered it; he had not returned, the provisions were untouched. It was a dreadful ending to our expedition. The mountains amongst which we had spent so many pleasant days together no longer were the same. The sunshine and the beauty were gone; savage, cruel, and inhospitable the black pinnacles of the ridges and the overhanging glaciers of cold ice filled my mind with only one thought. I could not stop at Astor. Moreover, by descending the valley I should at least meet Hastings sooner, for he was returning by forced marches to join me at Astor. On the 6th September we met at Doian. Beyond what he had already told me in his telegram there was nothing.

Together we returned to Astor to arrange our future movements. There we agreed that it was necessary to return to the Diamirai nullah at once, and together explore the upper part of the valley beyond the high camp. Provisions and ponies were hastily got, and after having arranged with Captain Stewart for as much help as possible, we started for the Diamirai by way of the Indus valley and the Bunar nullah.

The first day's march down the Astor valley brought us to Doian. There we were hospitably received by the officers of the Pioneer regiment, who, earlier in the year under Colonel Kelly, had marched over the Shandur pass to the relief of Chitral.

Below Doian the road descends rapidly by zig-zags towards the Astor stream: soon all vegetation is left behind, and one enters a parched and barren land. The valley is hemmed in by precipitous cliffs on both sides, and the road in many places has been hewn and blasted out of the solid rock. Bones of horses strew the wayside, and occasionally a vulture will sail by. The heat becomes oppressive, and the glare from the hillsides down which no water runs suggests a mountainous country in the Sahara.

Before this road was built, the old path led over the summit of the Hatu Pir, and the traveller now misses a marvellous view of Haramosh, Rakipushi, and the Indus valley by plunging down into this bare, desolate nullah, shut in on all sides by precipitous hills.

The small post of Ramghat, or Shaitan Nara, where this road finally emerges from the Astor nullah into the great valley of the Indus, is merely a post for guarding the suspension-bridge across the Astor stream. Here are stationed some Kashmir troops, and here it is that the roads to Chilas and Gilgit separate.

The Chilas road follows down the Indus on the left bank, through a country which probably has no equal in the world. How this astounding valley was formed it is difficult to say; but the valley is there, and a wilder, grander, more desolate, and more colossal rift cannot occur elsewhere on the earth's surface.

'Is this the scene
Where the old Earthquake-dæmon taught her young
Ruin?'

From the summit of Nanga Parbat to the waters of the Indus below is in depth nearly 24,000 feet. On the opposite side, the naked hillsides rising in precipice after precipice are entirely barren of all vegetation. Waterworn into innumerable gullies and rock towers, they present a melancholy and arid appearance; and, although their summits are 12,000 feet above the Indus, they do not form a north side to this gorge in any way comparable with that on the south. The floor of the valley is filled with the debris of countless Himalayan deluges, yet the Indus looks like a small and dirty stream. To appreciate in any way the gigantic scale of the whole is quite impossible. What is the depth of that stealthily flowing flood and the measure of its waters, who can say? For it is more than six hundred miles from its source, and its tributaries sometimes are almost as big as itself. From the borders of Swat and Chitral, from the Darkot pass, from the Kilik beyond Hunza, and from the Hispar pass, the waters collect to form the Gilgit river, one only of the many tributaries of the Indus. This tract of the Mustagh range is nearly two hundred miles long by eighty broad. The Shigar river drains the waters from the Mustagh range and K^2, perhaps the greatest accumulation of ice and snow that exists outside the arctic regions. The Nubra and Shayok rivers collect their waters from a yet larger area. But still east of all these tributaries, the Indus itself rises three hundred miles away in those unknown lands of Tibet behind the Himalaya and near the source of that mysterious river of eastern India, the Bramaputra. Yet all these collected waters are penned into this apparently slow flowing and narrow river, as with silent but stealthy haste it twists and turns through the gigantic chasm at the base of Nanga Parbat. Once, not many years ago, in December 1840, into the upper end of this gorge the side of the Hatu Pir fell, forming a dam probably over 1000 feet high.[1] A lake was formed behind it for miles. The water rose to the level of Bunji fort, 300 feet above the river below, and up the Gilgit valley this lake, newly formed, reached nearly to Gilgit itself. For six months the waters were held back till, topping the vast accumulation, they burst the dam, 'and rushed in dark tumult thundering.' The lake is said to have emptied in one day. A small remnant of the barrier can still be seen near Lechre on the Chilas road.

[1] See note, p. 305.

The heat in this valley is so great after eleven o'clock in the day, that it is impossible to travel, and makes it necessary to seek what shade there may be till the sun has sunk low in the sky. The naked rocks glisten and tremble in the heat, the staring colours of the parched hillsides, and the intense glare of the sun in this desert land, are in curious contrast to the shady valleys that lie thousands of feet up, hidden away in the recesses of the great mountain. But it is after the evening shadows have one by one lengthened, after the last glow of the hot orange sunset has at last faded out of the sky, and from out the darkness the rising moon lights up this deserted landscape with mysterious shadows and perplexing distances, that the whole scene becomes totally beyond description. The intricacy of form shown by the silent mountains seem to be some magnificent and great imagination from the mind of a Turner. The white moonlight, and the grotesque black shadows and leering pinnacles piercing the starlit sky, can only belong to a land dreamt of by a Gustave Doré as a fitting illustration to the Wandering Jew, and only be described by Shelley :—

'At midnight
The moon arose: and lo! the ethereal cliffs
Of Caucasus, whose icy summits shone
Among the stars like sunlight, and around

> Whose caverned base the whirlpools and the waves
> Bursting and eddying irresistibly
> Rage and resound for ever.'

But without doubt the dominant sensation in this strange land is that of fear and abhorrence; and what makes it all the more appalling is that this thing before one is there in all its nakedness; it has no reserve, there is nothing hidden. Its rugged insolence, its brutal savagery, and its utter disregard of all the puny efforts of man, crushes out of the mind any idea that this spot belongs to an ordinary world.

Whether in the day or the night it is the same. During the stifling hours of noon the valley sleeps in the scorching sunlight, but there, always there, is that monstrous flood below, slowly, ceaselessly moving. Occasionally the waters will send up an angry and deep-tongued murmur, when some huge eddy, rising to the surface, breaks, and belches out the waters that have come from the lowest depths.

At night in the stillness and the heat, as one lies unable to sleep, imagination runs riot; from out the inky shadows that seam the hill-sides in the pale moonlight, dragons and great creeping monsters seemingly appear crawling slowly down to drink at the ebon flood beneath. And imagination easily in restless dreams becomes reality, thus adding tenfold to the already accumulated horrors. But at last in the darkness—

> 'Before the phantom of false morning dies'—

suddenly a breath of cold air, as from heaven, descends like a splash of cool water. It has wandered down from the upper snows. Then a few moments later comes another; and, tired out, real sleep claims one at last.

Later, when one awakes, the morning sun has risen, sending his light slanting across the hillsides with a promise that before he sets we may be delivered from the bottom of this singular abyss. No description, however, can possibly give an adequate idea of the immensity, the loneliness, and the feeling of the insignificance of human affairs that is produced by this valley of the Indus below Rhamghat.

It was not till the 13th that we reached Bunar Post, a small station for troops at the bottom of the Bunar nullah. Here we were met by Captain de Vismes, who was in command of the Chilas district. He had most kindly come from Chilas to help us with coolies up the Bunar nullah, and from there to the Diamirai nullah. From Bunar Post to our destination it took no less than three days' hard travelling; for as I have already pointed out, it is not possible to go straight up the valley. If we had been able to travel direct, it meant an ascent of some 9000 feet, but by the only possible route that existed, nearly double that height had to be climbed before we finally, on the 16th, found ourselves once more in the Diamirai nullah. What a change, however, met our gaze! The great masses of wild rose-trees that had welcomed us on our first visit were bare even of leaves. The willow groves now lifted gaunt, leafless branches into the chill air, and sighed mournfully when the cold wind shook them, and the rhododendrons were powdered with snow. Winter had set in, as the Chilas herdsmen had warned us it would, only a month before; and the contrast was all the more marked when compared with the temperature of nearly 100° in the shade, which existed a few miles away by the Indus.

Hastings and I soon saw that any attempt at exploration amongst the higher glaciers was out of the question. We went up the glacier as far as half-way to the old upper camp where the provisions had been found untouched, but even there it was wading through snow nearly a foot deep; ultimately we climbed through heavy powdery snow, perhaps 500 feet up the south side of the valley, to obtain a last look at the valley in which Mummery, Ragobir, and Goman Singh had perished. The avalanches were thundering down the face of Nanga Parbat, filling the air with their dust; and if nothing else had made it impossible to penetrate into the fastnesses of this cold, cheerless, and snow-covered mountain-land, they at least spoke with no uncertain voice, and bade us be gone. Slowly we descended, and for the last time looked on the great mountain and the white snows where in some unknown spot our friends lay buried.

But although Mummery is no longer with us, though to those who knew him the loss is irreparable, though he never can lead and cheer us on up the 'gaunt, bare slabs, the square, precipitous steps in the ridge, and the bulging ice of the gully,' yet his memory will remain—he will not be forgotten. The pitiless mountains have claimed him—and—amongst the snow-laden glaciers of the mighty hills he rests. 'The curves of the wind-moulded cornice, the delicate undulations of the fissured snow,' cover him, whilst the 'grim precipices, the great brown rocks bending down into immeasurable space,' and the snow-peaks he loved so well, keep watch, and guard over the spot where he lies.

THE CANADIAN ROCKY MOUNTAINS

> 'A land of streams! some, like a downward smoke,
> Slow-dropping veils of thinnest lawn, did go:
>
> . . . . . .
>
> They saw the gleaming river seaward flow
> From the inner land: far off, three mountain-tops,
> Three silent pinnacles of aged snow,
> Stood sunset-flushed.'
>
> *The Lotos-Eaters.*

FAR away in the west of North America, west of the Great Lakes, west of Lake Winnipeg, west of the endless prairie, lies a 'Great Lone Land': a land almost bare of inhabitants, a land deserted, if we except a few prospectors, trappers, and wandering Indians who spend their time amongst the mountain fastnesses, either hunting wild animals or searching for gold and minerals.

Looking at a map of North America, one sees how a vast range of mountains stretches from far south in the United States to Alaska, more than two thousand miles away. This backbone of a continent in reality is made up of a series of ranges, running parallel with one another. In Canada there are, roughly, only two: the Rocky Mountains to the east, and the Cascade range to the west, forming the shore of the Pacific Ocean. In breadth about five hundred miles, in length over fifteen hundred, if one includes the continuation of the Cascade range into Alaska, where are situated the highest mountains in North America: Mount St. Elias, 18,090 feet, Mount Logan, 19,539 feet, and Mount M'Kinley (at the head waters of the Shushitna river), 20,874 feet. Much of this country still has 'unexplored' printed large across it, and until a few years ago, when a trans-continental railway connected the Atlantic with the Pacific Ocean, parts of the western portion of the Dominion of Canada, stretching as it does for thousands of miles, covered with dense forests, watered by unnumbered rivers, was as difficult of access as Siberia.

The magnitude of the Dominion, even at the present day, is hard to realise. It can only be appreciated by those who have travelled through its mighty woods, over its vast lakes and prairies, and explored the fastnesses of those lonely canyons of the West. Halifax, in Nova Scotia, is nearer to Bristol than to Vancouver on the Pacific coast, and Klondike is further north of Vancouver than Iceland is of London. Since, however, the Canadian-Pacific Railway has bridged the continent, these mountain solitudes of the Far West are much more accessible to the ordinary traveller, and the wild, secluded valleys of the Canadian Rocky Mountains are becoming more frequented by sportsmen and mountaineers. It does not need a prophet to foretell their future. A land where the dark green valleys are filled with primeval forest, where the pine, spruce, and fir, poplars, white maple, and cedar, vie with each other in adding colour to the landscape and beauty to the innumerable rivers, lakes, and streams: a land where endless snow-clad mountains send up their summits into the clear air from great glaciers below, where ridges of crags, pinnacles of rock, and broken mountain-side, catch sometimes the glow of the early dawn or the sunset, or at others bask in the glare of the midday heat, changing their colour perpetually from grey to crimson, from gold to purple, whilst below always lie the mysterious dark pine woods, filled with scents of the trees, and the noise of the wind as it sighs amongst the upper branches: such a land can only be employed by man for one purpose, it must become a playground where the tired people can make holiday.

It must become the Switzerland of North America, and, like Switzerland, no doubt, some day will be completely overrun; at present, however, the valleys are unspoilt; wild, beautiful, untouched and unscarred by the hand of man. Fortunately the

Canadian Rocky Mountains never can be the centre of any great manufacturing district; and as they are in extent vastly greater than the Alps, for a very long time to come they will remain the hunting ground for those who care to spend their spare time in breathing pure air, and in living amidst splendid scenery.

At the present time the exploration of these mountains is going rapidly forward, at least in those portions near where the Canadian-Pacific Railway passes through them; and the mountaineer of to-day is offered great opportunities. For should he climb to the summit of any peak, even near the railway, high enough to give an extensive view, by far the greater number of the mountains and peaks that can be seen stretching in every direction, as far as the eye can see to the horizon, are as yet untrodden by human feet.

The approach also to this splendid range is exceptionally fine. From the east, as the traveller leaves Winnipeg and enters on the prairie, till he reaches the foot of the mountains at Morley, nearly nine hundred miles away, the broad endless spread of the open country is seen. On many this apparently desolate, never-ending expanse of rolling grassland produces a sensation of weariness. But it is like the open sea in its size, and, like the ocean, has a charm that ordinary country does not possess. Its very immensity gives a mystery to it: sometimes the air is clear as crystal, and the white clouds on the horizon seem to be touching some far-distant fold of the landscape; at others the plain dances in the heat, and great mirage lakes can be seen covering the middle distances; again, thunder-storms pass along the sky, whose piled masses of cumuli clouds send down ribbons of fire, often causing fires that sweep for miles over the open grassland. At early dawn and sunset, however, are produced the great scenic effects of the prairie, and to look down the sky from the zenith to the setting sun, a great red ball just disappearing below the horizon, and count the colours that light up the islands, bays, promontories, and continents of that marvellous cloudland, makes one forget that one is in a railway train, or has anything to do with everyday life; it is like actually seeing for the first time some fairyland that one has read of in one's childhood. Afterwards, when the full moon comes out, the distances seem almost greater, and one can lie comfortably in bed and gaze at the landscape sliding swiftly by, comparing the ease and rapidity of modern travel, which does hundreds of miles in one night, with that of the pioneers who first traversed these endless plains a century or more ago.

Near a station called Gleichen, the Rocky Mountains can be seen more than one hundred miles away, but it is not till one approaches them that it is recognised how abruptly they rise out of the prairie, like a long wall, with apparently not an opening; and, even when a few miles away, they seem an impenetrable barrier. The railway, however, follows the bank of the Bow river, which from its size must at least come down a moderate-sized valley, and just above where the Kananaskis, a side river, is crossed, a sudden bend of the line takes one through the gateway of the hills and the Bow valley is entered, which is then followed westward up to the Great Divide, or watershed, sixty miles away.

The approach to the Rocky Mountains from the Pacific coast is through country of a totally different nature. From Vancouver to the Great Divide is five hundred miles; along the whole of this distance the railway line is surrounded by the most splendid mountain scenery. At first the line runs up the great and broad valley of the Fraser river, which when seen in the light of a fine September afternoon is magnificent. For it is shut in on all sides by high mountains (one, Mount Baker, being 14,000 feet), and filled with such timber as only grows on the Pacific coast, all of it the natural forest, vast Douglas firs of giant girth, cedars, poplars, and maples, with their autumn-colouring of crimson, green, and gold, adding beauty to this lovely valley; whilst winding backwards and forwards across it, flows the vast flood of the Fraser. Certainly it is one of the finest large valleys I have ever seen. Then further up is the world-famous Fraser canyon, not so beautiful as the greater valley below, but grand and terrible in its own way. There are fiercer and bigger rivers and gorges in the Himalaya. Here it is that for over twenty miles the railway track has been hewn in many places out of the solid wall of the canyon, whilst below rush the pent-up waters of the great river, sometimes slowly moving onwards with only the occasional eddy coming up to the surface to show the depth of water, again rushing with wildest tumult between narrow walls of black rock, tossing up the spray, and foaming along, afraid that unless it hastened madly through its rock-girt channel the almost overhanging walls, hundreds of feet high, would fall in and prevent it ever getting down to the open sea. Leaving the valley of the Fraser, the railway follows the desolate gorge of the Thompson river, and after passing through a series of minor mountains, comes down to the valley of the Columbia river, which here is running almost due south. If it had been possible to have built the line up the Columbia valley to the Rocky Mountains, no doubt that route would have been followed, but the railway has been taken over the Selkirk range instead. It is whilst crossing the Selkirks that by far the most wonderful part of this mountain line is to be seen. From the Columbia to the summit there is a rise of 2800 feet, and the descent on the other side to the Columbia river again is 1775 feet in less than twenty miles. Here are to be seen the miles of snow-sheds through which the train has to go, whilst towering into the sky are all the white snow-peaks of the Selkirks, and the glaciers that almost come down to the railway itself.

From the Columbia to the Great Divide another ascent has to be made, this time of 2800 feet, and the last 1250 feet of this is done in the short distance of ten miles. It is not in any way exaggerating to say that these five hundred miles of line give by far the most extensive and varied wild mountain scenery that can be obtained from any railway train in the world. The Fraser valley, and canyon, the Selkirk Mountains, and the scenery of the Rocky Mountains, before the Great Divide is reached, are each one of them wonderfully beautiful, and each one of them possesses so much individuality of its own, that to forget the impressions they make would be impossible.

The Great Divide is at the watershed, or on the top of the Kicking Horse pass. One of the most curious features of the Canadian Rocky Mountains is the lowness of the passes, also their number. The average height of the mountains is between 10,000 and 11,000 feet, yet none of these passes are much over 6000 feet, so that the simplest way to describe the range is to take the various masses of mountains that lie between the passes.

Twenty miles south of the Kicking Horse pass lies first the Vermilion pass (5265 feet), next comes the Simpson pass (6884 feet), thirteen miles further south, thus giving three groups of mountains which can be named as follows :—

(1) *The Temple group* (or Bow range); and *the Goodsir group* (or Ottertail range).

This group is south of the Kicking Horse pass and north of the Vermilion pass.

(2) *The Ball group*, which lies south of the Vermilion pass and north of the Simpson pass.

(3) *The Assiniboine group*, which lies south of the Simpson pass.

North of the Kicking Horse pass the peaks and glaciers of the Rocky Mountains have been more carefully explored and for a greater distance than on the south side of the railway. It will be sufficient, however, only to mention the passes through the mountains which are to be found in that tract of country (120 miles long), lying south of the Athabasca pass, and north of the Kicking Horse pass. The first pass across the Rocky Mountains is the Howse pass, 4800 feet, and thirty miles north of the railway; thirty miles further north is the Thompson pass, 6800 feet; next comes Fortress Lake pass, thirty-five miles distant, and only 4300 feet high; and lastly, twenty-five miles further, still to the north, the Athabasca pass, 5700 feet. Thus if we omit the mountains north of the Athabasca pass, there are four more groups. Taking them in order, they are:—

(4) *The Balfour group* (or Wapta range), lying between the Kicking Horse pass and the Howse pass.

(5) *The Forbes group*, lying between the Howse pass and the Thompson pass.

(6) *The Columbia group*, lying between the Thompson pass and the Fortress Lake pass.

(7) *The Mount Hooker group*, lying between the Fortress Lake pass and the Athabasca pass.

In the Temple-Goodsir group, which is situated just to the south of the Canadian Pacific Railway, are a very large number of rock- and snow-peaks; in fact, probably more varied rock climbing can be

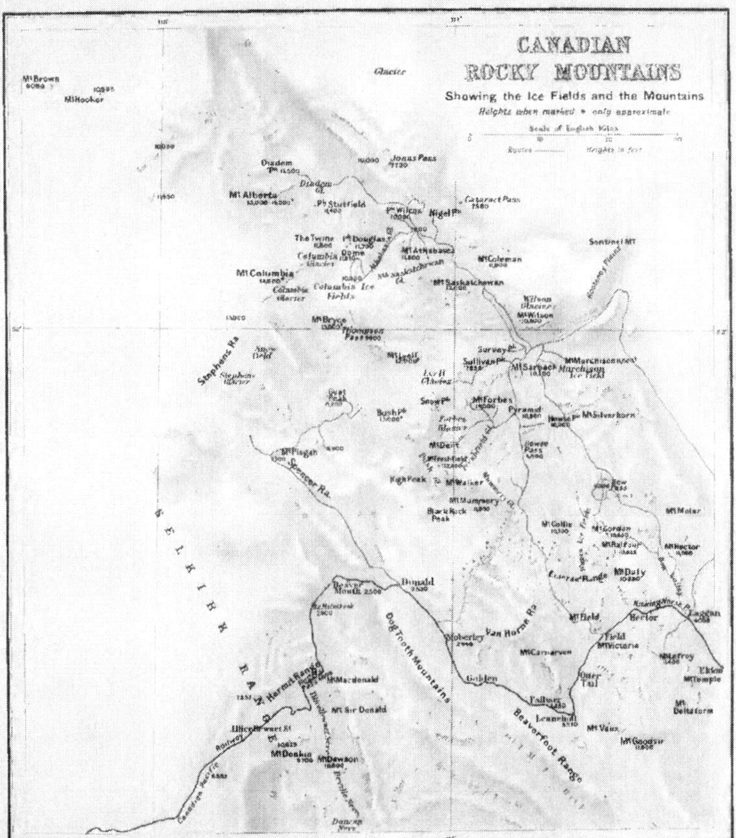
CANADIAN
ROCKY MOUNTAINS
Showing the Ice Fields and the Mountains
Mt Columbia
Mt Alberta
Diadem Pk
Jonas Pass
Nigel Pk
Mt Athabasca
Mt Coleman
Mt Saskatchewan
Columbia Ice Fields
Sentinel Mt
Mt Bryce
Survey Pk
Sullivan Pk
Mt Sarback
Mt Forbes
Bush Pk
Mt Pisgah
Spencer Ra.
Stephens Ra
Mt Silverhorn
Bow Pass
Mt Collie
Mt Gordon
Mt Balfour
Mt Hector
Mt Daly
Donald
Beaver Mouth
Dog Tooth Mountains
Van Horne Ra
Moberley
Golden
Mt Field
Field
Mt Victoria
Laggan
Mt Lefroy
Mt Temple
Mt Carnarvon
Mt Macdonald
Mt Sir Donald
Mt Donkin
Mt Dawson
Mt Vaux
Mt Goodsir
Beaverfoot Range
Leanchoil
Palliser
S E L K I R K R A N G E
Canadian Pacific Railway

found here than in any of the other groups of mountains. Mounts Temple, Lefroy, Victoria, Stephen, Cathedral, Vaux, and the Chancellor have all been ascended, but Goodsir, Hungabee, and Deltaform, all of them first-class peaks, yet wait for the first party to set foot on their summits. Besides the numerous good mountain climbs that can be found in this district, many most charming lakes and pine-clad valleys lie hidden away in the narrow valleys. It would be hard to find in any mountain-land a more perfect picture than that afforded by Lake Louise, a clear, deep lake, surrounded by pine woods and snow-clad peaks whose reflection in the water seems almost more natural than the reality in the distance. The O'Hara lakes and Paradise valley also possess the wild grandeur and rich fertility that is one of the chief attractions of the Rocky Mountains of Canada.

Of the Mount Ball group nothing need be said, Mount Ball being the only peak in it which reaches 11,000 feet. As seen from the summit of Mount Lefroy, Mount Ball is a long, somewhat flat-topped mountain covered with ice and snow. Perhaps, however, on the southern side it may be more precipitous and rocky. In the Assiniboine group there seems only one important mountain, Mount Assiniboine itself. But what is wanting in quantity is certainly atoned for by the excessive grandeur and beauty of Mount Assiniboine. For long called the Canadian Matterhorn (11,830 feet), it towers a head and shoulders above its fellows, the highest peak south of the line. For several years it withstood many determined attempts made to scale its sharp, pyramid-shaped summit; but in August of 1901 the Rev. J. Outram, with two Swiss guides, was fortunate enough at last to conquer this difficult mountain.

The chief feature of the Balfour group is the great expanse of upper snow-fields on the Wapta névé. The highest peak, Mount Balfour, 10,873 feet, was ascended in 1898 by Messrs. Charles S. Thompson, C. L. Noyes, and C. M. Weed. Once on this central reservoir of ice none of the peaks are difficult to climb. The Bow river, which has its source at the north-eastern corner of this Wapta snow-field, flows down the Bow valley, which skirts for more than twenty-five miles the eastern slopes of the Balfour group. This Bow valley is an excellent example of the numberless valleys that are to be found amongst the Rocky mountains, flat-bottomed and filled with pine woods and marshes or muskegs. Two beautiful lakes, the Upper and Lower Bow lakes, filled with trout, give good sport to the fisherman; but to fish successfully a raft must be built, for there are no boats as yet on the lakes. The Upper Bow lake is particularly beautiful, for in many places on its shores are great expanses of open grassland, covered here and there with clumps of dwarf rhododendron bushes, or, it may be, studded with thickets of pine and other trees, whilst on the opposite shore the mountains rise sheer for several thousand feet, and more than one glacier hangs poised high up on the cliffs, above the clear blue water beneath.

The next group further north, the Forbes group, has not been visited as yet by many mountaineering parties. But it contains possibly the highest peak in the Canadian Rocky Mountains, Mount Forbes, which is certainly considerably over 13,000 feet, and may be as much as 14,000 feet high. The Bush peak and Mount Freshfield also must be about 12,500 to 13,000 feet, and Mount Lyell is not much less, perhaps 12,000 feet. Many ice-fields lie underneath these high peaks: the Freshfield, Bush, and Lyell snow-fields being the most important. In this group as yet none of the peaks have been ascended, and up to the present only on the Freshfield glacier has any one set foot. This is largely due to the difficulty of getting to the foot of the peaks and the time necessary to expend on such an expedition. To get to the bottom of Mount Forbes from Laggan, the nearest spot on the Canadian-Pacific railway, would take about nine days, and, should the Saskatchewan be in full flood, it might take four or five days more.

The Columbia group, which is still further north, was only discovered in 1898 by Messrs. Stutfield, Woolley, and myself. It is by far the biggest accumulation of glaciers that we have yet seen, covering an area of at least one hundred square miles; moreover, from a geographical point of view, it claims additional interest, for it is the source of the two great rivers, the Athabasca, the Saskatchewan, and formerly probably of the Columbia as well. The mountains also that rise out of these untrodden snow-fields are amongst the highest peaks in the Canadian Rocky Mountains, with the one exception of Mount Forbes. At present it is impossible to say with certainty whether Mount Columbia or Mount Forbes is the higher. Personally I should like to give the preference to Mount Columbia. Another peak situated near the centre of this group, the Dome, 11,650 feet, on whose summit we stood in 1898, is the only mountain in North America the snows of which when melted feed rivers that flow into the three oceans—the Atlantic, the Arctic, and the Pacific. North of

The Freshfield Glacier

Mount Columbia another peak was discovered, Mount Alberta, over 13,000 feet. This mountain, unlike Mount Columbia, is a rock-peak and flat-topped. Its summit is ringed round with tremendous precipices, and its north-western face must be particularly grand, for it rises straight from the valley of the Athabasca for nearly 8000 feet.

The outlets from the great Columbian ice-field are very numerous; and many large glaciers flow into the valleys to feed the head waters of the Saskatchewan, the Athabasca, and the tributaries of the Columbia.

Of the mountains in the next group further north practically nothing is known. Only three parties in modern times have even penetrated into the valleys of this land south of the Athabasca pass—Professor Coleman (1893), during his search for Mounts Hooker and Brown; and Wilcox (1896) and E. Habel (1901). It is improbable that there are any peaks as high as 13,000 feet, but many covered with ice, snow, and glaciers were seen from the summits of the Dome and Diadem peak in 1898, when we were on the Columbian ice-fields. That this mountain-land remains unexplored is not to be wondered at, for the country is so far away, and so difficult to get at, from any human habitation that it takes weeks of hard work battling with the rivers and forests before even the valleys are reached which lie at the bottom of these ranges of snow- and glacier-covered mountains.

When one has got accustomed to it, however, travelling in these vast mountain solitudes becomes by no means either irksome or unpleasant. But before one is capable of understanding all the woodcraft and knowledge requisite for successfully guiding a party through the endless forested valleys, the apparent monotony is apt to weary the traveller; afterwards, however, when a thousand and one things in the woods or on the mountain-side are for the first time seen and understood, then the environment no longer dominates one. For instance, a peculiar notch or 'blaze' on an occasional tree means that some prospector or Indian has been there before, or perhaps a newly overturned stone amongst the moss tells how a bear has recently been searching for food; or, again, some half-obliterated mark by the side of a stream means cariboo, or, if higher up, goat or the wild sheep. Then, often by the kind of tree one can roughly guess how high one is, for certain poplars, for instance the balsam poplar, I have never seen higher than 5000 feet.

Of course amongst the Canadian Rockies it is

necessary on every expedition to take men and horses. The men are to look after the horses and the camp, and to cut the trail. The horses carry the food or 'grub-pile,' the tents, etc.

At first one is quite unaccustomed to the leisurely method of progression, and quite unacquainted with many mysterious things that afterwards appear obvious. Now that I look back on my first day with ponies in the Rockies I blush for my incompetence and ignorance.

To begin with, we were late in starting—our men, with most of the ponies and heavy baggage, had gone up the Bow valley, leaving us three ponies for the remainder of the luggage. At the very start, if it had not been for the help of an obliging man at Laggan railway station, I do not think we should ever have satisfactorily tied on all the odd packages. To pack an Indian pony, and finish all off neatly with a good tight diamond hitch, is an accomplishment not possessed by every one. After three summers' experience I really now can tie it: at least I know I could, but it is a wonderful hitch; and although you think that you have got it all right, when you begin to pull the rope tight, somehow it all comes undone and one must start again from the beginning.

The ponies having been packed, we started, but

soon lost our way amongst the most dreadful tangle of fallen timber; the men had 'blazed' the way, but we were new at the work, and so soon got out of the trail. After getting the ponies with great difficulty through some miles of this timber, we gradually worked ourselves free, getting into more open ground, but it was out of Scylla into Charybdis, for now it was a question of how to get through endless swamps or muskegs that filled up the floor of the valley. Here the blazes of course stopped, and soon we missed the tracks of the other horses and got hopelessly lost, floundering about in every direction trying to find a way through.

Several times the luckless ponies, dead tired and overladen, had sunk up to their bellies, but with terrified snorts and plunges had just managed to get out again. At last the sun went down, then daylight disappeared, and finally the moon came out, and we were still in that swamp. Ultimately we tried to make for the forest at the side of the valley, but one of the horses got so deep into a hole that only with difficulty we managed to prevent him vanishing altogether. He was at last rescued with an Alpine rope; and we also were rescued from a night out in a swamp by our headman, Peyto, who had come down the valley to look for us. The horses had to be left for the night, but we, wading through everything, got safely into camp at about midnight. These Indian ponies are wonderfully clever in thick timber or in the streams and rivers that have every now and then to be crossed.

One old grey that I rode for two different trips was a most wise old animal, rather stiff in the knees, but wonderfully sure-footed, and never once did he even brush my leg against a tree trunk even in the thickest timber. He was also a very gentlemanly old animal, never frightened (unless he got into a muskeg), never in a hurry, very fond of going to sleep, also of having his own way, and his way was usually the right one.

To those who wish to spend all their time, during a short holiday, climbing peaks, the Canadian Rocky Mountains cannot be recommended without some explanation. Firstly, they are a very long way off; and secondly, many of the finest groups, lying, as they do, perhaps fifty or a hundred miles from the railway, necessitate days of travel with ponies, provisions, etc., before even their base is reached. Still undoubtedly the pleasure of the leisurely advance through the charming valleys and dense pinewoods is to

> 'Those who love the haunts of Nature,
> Love the shadow of the forest,
> Love the winds among the branches,
> And the rain-shower and the snowstorm,
> And the rushing of great rivers'

of quite an equal importance to the joys of a first ascent.

The absolutely free life that one experiences in camp never palls, let the weather be good or bad; as one jumps out of one's sleeping-bag into the fresh morning air, one is always ready for the day's work.

Perhaps it is a glorious morning. The men have gone off to find the ponies, which, if they have strayed far afield during the night, can be found by listening for the tinkle of the bell always tied to the neck of the bell-mare. Then after a breakfast of porridge, bacon, and whatever else there may be, the horses are packed—an operation which is hard work, and takes perhaps the best part of two hours when there are over a dozen horses to load. Each pack has to be finally tied on with the diamond hitch, otherwise in a very short time the pack would work loose, and, if once lost bit by bit in the dense undergrowth of the forest, would never be recovered.

Then comes the start, and the cavalcade files off into the virgin forest, led by the headman, whose business it is to pick out a trail amidst the dense undergrowth and the fallen trees along which the pack train can go. Soon the sound of the axe is heard, and the single file of ponies comes to a standstill whilst some fallen tree which bars the way is cut through. Sometimes the path leads along the bank of a swiftly flowing, muddy white river, swollen by the melting snows of the glaciers, which every now and then are seen through more open parts of the forest, glaciers that glimmer and shine high up amongst the peaks that wall in the valley below. It is in places such as this that the greatest danger to the horses and baggage is experienced. The banks of the river may be rotten, or a horse more self-willed than the others may suddenly plunge into the water, and often it is next to impossible to prevent others following; so that in one moment of time perhaps half the outfit may be sweeping down stream to perdition, and the expedition ruined by being left provisionless. Fortunately, although I have often seen our horses helplessly drifting down rivers that at first sight seemed hopeless to get out of, owing to the undercut banks, depth of water, and strength of current, yet somehow or other these plucky little ponies always have managed to scramble out again.

The silent forests, through which one sometimes has to march for days together, are not so dense, and the trees are not so large on the eastern side of the Divide as on the western, that is to say, in the valleys leading to the Columbia river.

In the valley of the Columbia itself, down which we travelled in 1900 from Donald to the Bush river, for several days we hardly saw the sky. The vast forest far surpassed in size anything we had seen on the other side of the range—huge pines, cotton-wood trees, firs, and spruces reaching to a height of 150 feet or more. The undergrowth too was very dense—cedar, white maple, and alder (near the streams), were found; whilst the fallen trunks of dead trees, sometimes six or eight feet in diameter, lay scattered with others of lesser size in every kind of position. Some in their fall had been arrested by others, and were waiting for the first gale to bring them crashing to the ground; whilst at the will of every breeze that wandered through the upper branches of the higher trees, these half-fallen monarchs of the forest would break the heavy stillness of the air by their complaints and groans against their more sturdy brethren for thus preventing them lying at peace upon the moss-covered ground below. Others that had lain perhaps scores of years in the wet underbush had decayed and rotted, leaving rich masses of decomposing vegetation, from which trees had sprung that in their turn also must fall and suffer the same change. There is a marvellous fascination about these quiet shady fastnesses of the western valleys. As one wanders day after day through this underworld, cut off from the glaring sun of noonday and the blue sky, hardly a sound breaks the stillness, whilst all around the ruin of ancient woods lies piled with a lavishness most absolute—that of Nature's self, the tangled wreck of a lifetime, the luxuriant growth of centuries.

It is in these western valleys that the rainfall is far greater than on the other side of the range, hence the forests are thicker and the muskegs and streams more dangerous. Only in the western valleys also is found that pest of British Columbia forests, the Devil's Club — a plant with large, broad leaves and a stem covered with spikes. Amongst the moist undergrowth it grows to a height of from five to six feet, trailing its stems in every direction and emitting a dank, unwholesome smell. Woe betide any one who with bare hand should roughly seize one of those stems, for the spikes enter the flesh, and, breaking off, produce poisoned wounds which fester. But whilst cutting trail it is impossible to prevent the long, twisted roots flying up occasionally, leaving their detestable thorns in all parts of one's body.

Sometimes instead of these virgin forests the trail—and this is especially true when one is near a pass at 6000 feet or 7000 feet—passes along wide expanses of meadow, with small rhododendron bushes and clumps of pines every here and there. Masses of flowers can be seen in every direction, many kinds of anemone, large yellow daisies, and many others. Near the watershed of a pass beautiful lakes of pure blue water are often found, and in a quiet summer afternoon the long slanting shadows and the reflection of pines, peaks, and glaciers lie still in the clear water. The contrast of colours often is almost dazzling. One instance in particular I shall never forget: it was in a valley thirty miles north of the line called Bear Creek, near two lakes where some years before a fire had burnt out several square miles of forest. The gaunt, shining black stems of the trees formed a curious but fitting background —shining like black satin—for the mass of brilliant golden yellow daisies that were in full bloom amongst the stones at their feet. There was no green of grass, in fact no other colour except that of the sky. This blaze of golden orange against satin black tree trunks, with a sapphire sky beyond, formed a contrast of colours but rarely seen in a landscape.

These burnt forests are one of the worst obstacles for delaying a party with horses. For a few years the ground is cleared excellently; but soon an undergrowth of pines springs up, then for many years the burnt dead trunks, which never seem to rot after having been charred by the fire, and the new thick undergrowth, make often a mile a day with a pack team good work. Often even without burnt timber to delay one, the progression up an unknown valley is very tedious. In 1900, whilst exploring the Bush valley on the western side of the mountains, our first view of the valley held out hopes to us that we should soon get to the head waters and the snow peaks fifteen miles away. Stretched out at our feet, as we looked down from a neighbouring hill, lay the valley, wide and level. There were no canyons or defiles that might necessitate lengthy détours up precipitous hillsides. The valley was open and flat. It is true we saw some muskegs at the sides, but along the level bottom stretched shingle flats, with streams all tangled together, looking like a skein of ravelled grey wool thrown down between the dull green hills, whilst the main river, winding first toward one hillside and then towards the other, sometimes branching, again reuniting, formed a veritable puzzle of interlacing channels, islands of pebbles, stretches of swamps, and small lakes all hopelessly intermingled. The first ten miles up that valley took us ten days' incessant work. Our way was alternately through immense timber, dense thickets of willows, through swamps, streams, small lakes, along insecure river banks, climbing up the hillsides, jumping logs, cutting through fallen trees and undergrowth so thick one could hardly see a yard ahead, splashing, fighting, and worrying ahead; we had an experience of almost everything that could delay us, and whether the woods, the streams, or the muskegs were worst, it was impossible to say.

So the days go by, and often real mountaineering is a luxury which has to be left till the last. But we were the pioneers; now the trails are partly made, and the way to get at the peaks is known, therefore the expenditure of time in arriving at any particular spot can be calculated with much greater certainty. But with this gain in time-saving comes also the lost pleasure of the uncertainty of an unknown land; now the country is being mapped and all the peaks are being named.

However, it will be many a long year before much real change can be made in the valleys that lie thirty or more miles from the line; also the snow peaks, the marvellously clear atmosphere, the woods, lakes, and scenery will remain the same. After a long day through these valleys of the Canadian Rocky Mountains one will be just as able to pitch one's tent and enjoy over the camp fire the stories of the hour, to eat one's dinner with the mountaineer's appetite, to smoke by the light of the smouldering logs, and to go to sleep safely, surrounded by these mysterious and dark forests.

I always think that the supreme moments of a mountaineer's existence are, more often, not whilst battling with the great mountains, but afterwards, when the struggle is done and the whole story is gone over again quietly by a camp fire. Violent action no doubt appeals to many people, but the delightful sense of content that wraps one round after a long and successful day on the mountains, after the victory has been won, is a very pleasant sensation. One such evening I remember in the Bush valley when no victory had crowned our efforts. We were returning, in fact, from an attempt to reach Mount Columbia which had proved an undoubted failure; still somehow I felt that although beaten, we had been honourably beaten, we had struggled hard, but two things had failed us—time and provisions—and we were retracing our steps towards civilisation. The camp that evening had been pitched on the banks of the Bush river. In the foreground, water and shingle stretched in desolate fashion westward to where ridges of dark pine woods sloped down from dusky peaks above, sending out point after point to strengthen the forms of the middle distance; whilst beyond, far away across the Columbia, the Selkirk mountains raised their snow peaks into the calm, clear sky, a mysterious land unexplored and unknown. Through a rift in the clouds in the far west shone the setting sun, tinging the dull grey clouds overhead and the stealthily flowing river below with its many-coloured fires. A faint evening breeze softly moved the upper foliage, a couple of inquisitive chipmunks were chattering near at hand, and a small stream could be heard whispering amongst the thickets near the banks of the river.

The great gnarled trunks of pine and fir, festooned with moss, fungi, and grey lichen, the dead, drooping branches, and the half fallen, decaying trunks propped up in dreary, melancholy array, caught for a moment the sunset's ruddy glow, whilst the mysterious shadows of the dense forest darkened by contrast. It was one of those evenings

> 'When, upon a tranced summer night,
> Those green robed senators of mighty woods,
> Tall oaks, branch charmed to the earnest stars,
> Dream, and so dream all night without a stir,
> Save from one gradual solitary gust,
> Which comes upon the silence, and dies off,
> As if the ebbing air had but one wave.'

Such evenings compensate one for many a wet, dreary day spent amongst the mountains. Nature suddenly offers them to the traveller without any toil on his part. He has only to sit watching, surrounded by the dark forest, the stretch of waters, and the ever-changing glory of the setting sun; then, unmindful of the worry of yesterday, or the uncertainties of to-morrow, amidst the great stillness, he feels with absolute conviction one thing and one thing only—that it is good to be alive and free. Civilised life no doubt teaches us much, but when one has once tasted the freedom of the wilds, a different knowledge comes. The battling with storm, rain, cold, and sometimes hunger, and the doubt of what any day may bring forth, these at least teach that life—that mere existence—is beyond all price.

THE ALPS

'Remember now thy Creator in the days of thy youth, while the evil days come not, nor the years draw nigh, when thou shalt say, I have no pleasure in them.'—*Ecclesiastes.*

MANY years ago I remember quoting once some paragraphs which seemed at the time to portray so exactly the attitude of certain people towards the Alps, that they were instantly plucked from their seclusion, for the purpose of enforcing some rather flippant and idle remarks of my own. These flippant efforts of mine, I may add, were not intended to be taken seriously. The paragraphs, however, were written in 1868, and can be found in the *Alpine Journal.*[1] I now presume to use them once more. 'So far as the Alps are concerned, we can now, I fear, expect nothing free altogether from the taint of staleness. For us the familiar hunting grounds exist no longer as they once existed.' Again: 'Those waters of oblivion which have overwhelmed the

[1] Vol. iv. p. 185.

Jungfraus and Finsteraarhorns of our youth.' And, 'It only remains for us to dally awhile with the best recollections of the now degraded mountains.'

As I have said, when I first quoted these sentences I did not believe one word of them. It is true that then I was younger and more enthusiastic; moreover, the Alps were new to me, and I was still able to appreciate to the full the beauties of that region of streams, glaciers, and snow peaks: then the sun still shone, then the morning and the evening, arrayed in their coat of many colours, called either to action or bid a cheerful good-night, and even then the fleeting clouds, flung abroad like 'banners on the outer wall,' would often make me stop and watch, till the mists dissolved into thin air left the high battlements of the mighty mountains once more clear against the blue sky. Yes! although I quoted these paragraphs, yet at that period, to me it was impious to question the sway of the monarchs of the earth. Degraded mountains, taint of staleness, waters of oblivion, Jungfraus overwhelmed, a truly depressing picture! but when one comes to examine into the real truth of the matter, the fact remains that the mountains are still there, and really after all in much the same condition as they were fifty years ago. Of course one must

A Crevasse on Mont Blanc

admit that many parts of Switzerland below the snow line and some infinitesimal bits higher up possibly have been degraded, but not by a natural process. This degradation is the work of the animal, Man; and it is difficult to say why he alone of all the inhabitants of this world, wherever he sets himself down, should always besmirch and befoul the face of Nature. Some literary and inquiring spirit should write a monograph on the subject.

What sight is more depressing than the gaunt, soot-begrimed trees that struggle for a pitiful existence around our centres of so-called civilisation? Where can a more squalid picture be either seen or imagined than a back slum in one of our manufacturing towns where the teeming millions are born, bred, and die? The inhabitants of a London back street never see this earth as Nature made it, beyond perhaps occasionally a green field. They know nothing of the great face of the world. What do mountains, streams, pinewoods, and lakes ruffled by the wind, mean to them? they only have seen the lower Thames and its mud banks. Expanses of heather moorland where the birds, the breezes, and the many summer scents wander to and fro: probably their nearest approach to these is Hampstead heath and oranges! The nations of the

East can teach Western civilisation several things, and the people of the Staffordshire Black Country would not lose were they to copy some of the methods of living in Japan.

Now the worst of all this is that as the nations expand and communication becomes easier, the several, as yet unspoilt, corners of the world, where man has not yet 'forked out' Nature, are in grave danger of being swept bodily into civilisation's net. Unfortunately the majority of mankind is hopelessly lacking in imagination, they are incapable of accommodating themselves to their environment, trying always instead to force their surroundings to fit their own small ideas.

Brighton becomes more civilised in direct ratio as it becomes more like London; and Switzerland—that is to say, where many unimaginative tourists go, and nowadays they go to most places from Lucerne to the tops of the highest mountains—is thus degraded. It becomes a herding place during August for the nations, each brings his own special atmosphere, his family, his newspaper, and himself. The money pours in, the state becomes civilised, and the hotels flourish. If Zermatt possessed first-class beer halls, a golf course, and plenty of motor cars, a very large number of the German, English, and French tourists would gladly amuse themselves each with his particular native pastime, and would never bother themselves about whether Monte Rosa was covered with ice and snow, or was merely a mud heap, or whether glaciers, Matterhorns, Dent Blanches were or were not.

It would be foolish to deny that the interest of mankind in man must necessarily be stronger than the mere abstract pleasure obtained from the contemplation of wild and beautiful scenery. So it follows that when a vast concourse gathers, such as is seen during the season at Zermatt, mankind naturally dominates the environment, and the study of man, not of scenery, prevails. This must be so. Take, for instance, any of our best novelists: of course they deal with people, not things. When Clive Newcome and J. J. (artists too, if you please) crossed the Alps, does Thackeray give us a long account of the scenery? Certainly not: the whole matter is disposed of at once, and in a sentence they are whisked from Baden to Rome. On the other hand, the descriptions of the beauties of Nature by Sir Walter Scott or by Wordsworth, who reads them now except with an occasional yawn? Far more interesting, and properly so too, are narratives of real, live people, their thoughts, their hopes, their disappointments. *Soldiers Three* appeals to every one; but should one begin to talk about the merits of Claude and Turner as painters of hills, and even quote some of Ruskin's very finest passages about Alps and Archangels, your neighbour at *table d'hôte* will either think that you are a great bore, or, perhaps, an extremely clever person; but will be far more interested, when the old lady opposite begins to tell how Mr. Jones was caught that very afternoon proposing to Miss Robinson, and how the Bishop of X. is really coming to stop at the hotel for a few days. All this is meant to show that by far the greater number of the hordes that invade Switzerland every year does not in reality take any interest at all, or at best a very feeble one, in the only really national dish that Switzerland has to offer. They neither care for it, nor do they understand it.

Naturally, therefore, the majority with their outside influence, with their own objects, ends, and atmosphere, entirely swamps the small remainder who appreciate the natural beauties of the land, and who fifty years ago practically held undivided possession. In those days the tourists, and they were few in the land, did not in the least mind suffering certain minor hardships owing to the absence of hotels: it was nothing compared with the pleasure that they obtained from the free life and the scenery; also, should they be mountaineers and scale some of the till then unvisited summits, on their descent into the valleys they were looked upon with wonder by the simple village folk and the herders of cattle of the small hamlets; these inhabitants would crowd round, when with arm extended and finger pointing to the distant peak of snow they described how yesterday, at such a time, they and their friend the chamois hunter of the district were on its summit. This sort of thing has most certainly gone, gone for ever. In this respect the Alps are as dead as Queen Anne—they have been overwhelmed in the waters of oblivion. The self-sufficient modern traveller now holds undivided sway in the chief central places of the Alps; and were it possible for him to impress his puny individuality on the great crags and the snow-fields of the mountains, to interfere with the colours of the sunset or the dawn, or to compel the clouds, then perhaps we might agree with the bitter cry of Ruskin, who, speaking of the artistic creative faculty of the present day, says that we 'live in an age of base conceit and baser servility—an age whose intellect is chiefly formed by pillage, and occupied in desecration; one day mimicking, the next destroying, the works of all noble persons who made its intellectual or art life possible to it: an age without honest confidence enough in itself to carve a cherry-stone with an original fancy, but with insolence enough to abolish the solar system, if it were allowed to meddle with it.'

Fortunately they cannot meddle with the mountains and the snow-fields. Still, as in those bygone days, man there is a mere speck. The peaks are as high and the snows as deep. Above, the glories of the sunset and the sunrise are the same, amidst the ice, the snow, and the black rocks; there the taint, and the adverse influence of this invasion of civilisation, is unfelt, although it may have overwhelmed the valleys below. The Jungfrau and the Finsteraarhorn still are as untouched and unspoiled, as far from vulgarisation as in the days when they were first conquered.

It is only when we descend from the mountains, and at the huts once more enter into contact with this other world, that the change begins to be felt, or when we have returned to our hotel, donned our dress clothes, and are seated before a bad imitation of a dinner, that we finally recognise that the waters of the great modern sea of vulgarity and mediocrity have engulfed us.

Forty years ago Switzerland, or at least the finest part of Switzerland, belonged to the tourist or traveller, call him which you will, who really cared for the healthy, out-of-door existence and the scenery; and to the mountaineer, who, as a rule, appreciated both the natural grandeur of the Alps, and at the same time the pleasure of spending his holidays high up amidst the ice and snow. At that time we find in the *Alpine Journal* (a record of mountain adventure) endless papers on the climbing and the exploration of the Alps. But if we examine the pages of the *Alpine Journal* of to-day, a distinct scarcity of papers on the Alps is at once apparent. In the year 1900, out of fourteen articles only five dealt with the Alps, for there nowadays exploration and new climbs are almost impossible. Moreover, records of mere mountain adventure without any description of an ascent of some unconquered peak have become too common. Therefore it is not remarkable that the mountaineer is driven further afield, preferring to win laurels amidst new ranges. But still the Alps are both broad and wide, and after all it is only along certain lines that the great civilised mob disports itself. It is true that all the mountains have been ascended, but surely that only destroys a minor attraction; moreover, fortunately almost anywhere on the Italian side of the watershed one is free from that lamentable state of affairs that obtains at such places as

Chamonix, Grindelwald, and Zermatt; and should the mountaineer possess a tent and a sleeping-bag he can always camp out, thus being entirely free. There are places on the south side of Mont Blanc, in the Rutor or in the Grand Paradiso district, in the Valpelline, and in many others, where delightful camps can be made and where one would hardly ever see a stranger for weeks together. There the mountaineer can live practically undisturbed in his own hunting ground of peaks, passes, and glaciers.

Amongst the most pleasant recollections I have of the Alps are those connected with our camps. We always had sleeping-bags, and I may say that during all the years I spent climbing with Mummery only twice have I slept in a hut with him.

There are few more pleasurable sensations than to be comfortable and warm under the lee of some great boulder, watching the stars as they slowly move westward; or to sit by a camp fire after the sun has set, and to recall all the enjoyment of the climb just finished; a feeling of most profound contentment with everything in the world steals over the party; the conversation becomes more and more disjointed as first one and then another turns over and sleeps.

When I look back and think of all the various

places where Mummery, Hastings, Slingsby, and I have slept out in the open, far away from the haunts of men, and remember how we enjoyed ourselves, I for one would go back year after year to the Alps if those times could be brought back again. In those days the glass of time, when shaken, ran in golden sands. Now all that is left of them is the memory.

It was in those days long ago, that I remember, how on one perfect evening at the beginning of August, we camped high up by the side of the Brenva glacier, having been well prepared for struggling with the tremendous southern face of Mont Blanc by the delightful dinners of M. Bertolini. The sun went down behind the Pétéret ridge—a ridge which always seems to me to be unsurpassed in the Alps—and we hoped that in another twenty-four hours we should be on the other side of the great mountain. But one of the great charms of mountaineering is its uncertainty, and instead of twenty-four it was forty-eight hours before we arrived at the Grands-Mulets. It would be distinctly perverting the truth to say that, at the time, we enjoyed the whole of our expedition, but often have I during winter evenings recalled that climb. I cannot now reproduce the unpleasant sensations, but the satisfaction and recollection of success becomes more pleasing as lapse of years adds enchantment to the memory of that fierce battle with Mont Blanc. I shall never forget how, hour after hour, Mummery, following a wrong direction of E. Rey's (who, as it turned out afterwards, had never been up Mont Blanc by this Brenva route), persistently kept towards the left; how at last the hard blue ice became so steep that it was almost impossible to cut steps in it; and how the ice also had a sticky feel when touched with the fingers, for we were in the shadow of the mountain.

Unfortunately we were 1500 feet from the summit; and as the daylight was only good for a few more hours, we had reluctantly to turn and make our way down that icy staircase. At one place where Hastings had thrown a portion of his breakfast into a small crevasse, we carefully recovered the discarded provisions, coming at last, just before darkness enveloped everything, to a small rock jutting out of that almost vertical face. The Brenva glacier was thousands of feet below us. One of the penalties of guideless climbing is that when prolonged step-cutting has to be undertaken, no amateur can compete with a first-class guide. Naturally, therefore, nights out on the mountains are often the price paid. Our penance on this particular expedition was to sit on that rock all night. The cold was intense, and it was not till the sun had risen next day that we were capable of moving. Once started, the blood began again to circulate, and keeping this time more to the right, a passage was forced with very great difficulty indeed through the almost overhanging edge of the great snow cap of Mont Blanc. In more than one place we had to use the axes forced home to their heads as a staircase for the first man. It was a magnificent climb, in fact the finest I have ever had. That ice world on the south side of Mont Blanc is on a larger scale than anything I know of outside the Himalaya. On the afternoon of the third day out from Courmayeur I arrived on the summit by crawling up on my hands and knees. But although the ascent had taken so long, the descent was accomplished much more expeditiously. In two hours we reached the Grands-Mulets. There, being supplied with omelette after omelette, I basely refused to roam any further; but Hastings and Mummery, unsatisfied, rushed down the remainder of the mountain, to lose themselves in the pine woods below in the darkness, reaching Couttet's and luxury late that night. If I was to recount all the splendid expeditions that we were taken by Mummery—how we sometimes failed, but much more often succeeded—this chapter could be made into a dozen; and yet, in spite of all these ascents, my knowledge of the Alps is extremely limited.

Curiously, however, I have found that sometimes those who most loudly complain of the Alps being played out are quite unacquainted with, or at least have never attempted, most of those ascents which it was my good fortune to make with Mummery. Certainly they were mostly made in the Mont Blanc range, a part which does not seem to commend itself so much to mountaineers of the present day as the eastern portion of the Alps. Yet where can be found anywhere else, in the whole range, rock pinnacles that are finer than the Aiguille Noire de Pétéret. Few people know that its west face is a sheer precipice of several thousand feet. In 1899 I was camping for a couple of days with Major Bruce and Harkabir Thapa, just opposite to it on the ridge between the Brouillard and Fresnay glaciers. It was then I watched a slab of rock fall from about twenty feet below the summit. It was a mass weighing perhaps fifty or a hundred tons. For over 1000 feet it touched nothing, then striking on a ledge it burst into a thousand fragments with a noise like thunder, and hardly one of the fragments touched rock again, but descended straight to the snows of the Fresnay glacier beneath.

We were investigating the south-west corner of Mont Blanc, intending if possible to make the ascent by the continuation of the Brouillard ridge. With this prospect in view, we ascended the Brouillard glacier to near the top of the Aiguille l'Innominata, but went no further. The Brouillard is a glacier that to try and descend on a hot summer afternoon would be foolish, to say the least of it. For, set at a very high angle, and broken up in the wildest fashion, although presenting a magnificent spectacle, it does not lend itself to safe mountaineering. Harkabir was much disappointed that we refused to go on, for he thought he could see his way up the rock escarpment at the head of the glacier, and, were that possible, probably no more difficulty would be met with from there to the summit. But in spite of the climber of the party being confident we could proceed, I as conductor insisted on turning back, being only a 'mere mountaineer.' One thing at least I was certain of: Bertolini lived at Courmayeur, not Chamonix, and forty-year old Barolo, together with countless other delicacies, was to be obtained from him alone. To return, however, from the excellences of the cuisine at Bertolini's to those of the range of Mont Blanc, should the jaded climber of 'degraded' mountains want more rock peaks, the ascent of the lesser Dru, in my opinion, can be repeated profitably. Not even amongst the Dolomites can one get the sensation of dizzy height and appalling depth to the same extent as on this mountain; moreover, there is a most sporting though small glacier to cross before one begins the rock ascent. Then the Charmoz and the Grépon are not to be despised. For a most varied climb, requiring every kind of mountain craft, the traverse of the Aiguille du Plan is to be recommended, from the Glacier des Pèlerins over the summit, down the Glacier du Plan, and back by the Glacier du Géant. Again, without doubt, the finest snow and ice climb in the Alps, surrounded the whole time by superb scenery, is from the Montanvert to the hut behind the Aiguille du Midi, thence over Mont Blanc du Tacul and the Mont Maudit to the summit of Mont Blanc, and down to the Grands-Mulets. Of course, I know that to recommend any one to climb Mont Blanc will certainly be regarded as a bold suggestion by those who have noticed a taint of staleness in the great mountains. For of all the peaks that have been overwhelmed by the waters of oblivion, surely Mont Blanc outrivals both the Jungfraus and the

Finsteraarhorns of the happy childhood of the Alps. Personally, however, I am a staunch adherent of the 'ancient monarch of the mountains.' But as Leslie Stephen says, the 'coarse flattery of the guide-books has done much to surround him with vulgarising associations.' Surely, though, Mont Blanc is far too magnificent, far too splendid to be much affected by such associations, and as if to shake them off every now and then, after he has been patted on the back by those of every nationality who swarm over his sides, he arises in his anger, hangs out his danger signal above his summit, and sweeps his glaciers and snows clear of the invading crowd. The Föhn wind and the angry clouds envelop him, his snow-fields glare with a ghastly dead white colour, and whirlwinds of clouds, snow, and gloom descend. But the storm passes, and once more he emerges clean and glistening in all his beauty.

But at Chamonix the Föhn wind of vulgarity seems to blow perpetually, enveloping always the great mountain in pale and dim eclipse, and obscuring the romance, the charm, and all honest appreciation of the old monarch. Fortunately one can easily run away, leaving this depressing atmosphere behind, and can bask once more in the sunshine, and camp amidst the unspoiled valleys near the snows.

Why there are not more mountaineers who take small tents to the Alps is always to me a mystery. For long ago most of the huts have become abominations, whilst the free life that is afforded by camp life adds a very great charm to mountain expeditions. Having tried it so often in the Himalaya, in Skye, in Norway, in the Canadian Rocky Mountains, and Switzerland, perhaps I may be biassed, but even if I never again had a chance of climbing a first-class peak in the Alps, I would return there to live the lazy, delightful, disreputable life in a tent, near the ice and the snows and the pine woods, to smell the camp fire, lie on my back all day amidst the grass and the flowers, listening to the wind, and looking at the sky and the great silent peaks. On the other hand, the idea of spending a month at Swiss hotels, arising in the darkness to wander forth in a bad temper, chilled to the bone, in order merely to finish off the remaining peaks of some district, so that I might say I had been up them all, and therefore never be bothered to return again—rather than perpetrate such a hideous waste of time I would go to some secluded spot on the western coast of these islands where the waves were for ever rolling in with that long, lazy, monotonous sweep that is only seen on the shores of the Atlantic, and there I would lie day after day on my back on the sands watching the ever-changing colours of the sea.

These things, however, can be done in their proper season, but until there are restaurants all over Mont Blanc, and railways up most of the peaks, illuminations of the Matterhorn every night by means of electricity and coloured fires, and all the avalanches are timed to be let loose only twice a day, namely at a morning and an afternoon performance—until that time arrives mountaineering in the Alps will still be worth while indulging in occasionally. Till then there will be plenty of space for the enthusiast who likes to wander amidst the snow- and ice-covered mountains. The ledges of rock high up, with the grey lichen on them, will still afford a resting-place from which the long glaciers far down below can be seen as they descend to the green-hued woods and the hazy valleys filled with sunshine. The overhanging cornices high above, for ever on the point of breaking off, will still hang poised in unstable equilibrium. The storms will sweep as frequently as of old across that mountain land, hiding for a brief space all in gloom; the lightning flashes, the roar of the thunder, the driving snow, and the keen biting wind will hunt the too presumptuous climber back to lower altitudes, as they have done often before; and afterwards the sun will again shine, dissolving the clouds, drying the lower slopes, and showing how the old mountains have once more put on a clean garment, which in magnificence, in glittering splendour, is as unmatched or unequalled as the deep, glowing colour of that 'solitary handmaid of eternity,' the open ocean, or the glories of the heavens at dawn or at sunset. Those who have learned to understand the language of the hills can appreciate the many-voiced calls of the mountains, and, I am sure, are not in the least afraid that, for the present, the Alps will be wholly ruined or degraded. For my own part, they will always possess an attraction which I care neither to analyse nor to destroy. I shall go back there just as the swallow at the end of summer goes south; and if by an unfortunate combination of circumstances anything should happen to prevent me ever returning from that world of snow, my ghost, could it walk, would then at any rate be surrounded by nothing common nor unclean, which might perhaps not be so should it be compelled to wander amongst the tombstones of a London cemetery.

THE LOFOTEN ISLANDS

> 'Near the outer lands of the silent mist,
>   The waves moan wearilie;
> Yet hidden there lie the Isles of the Blest,
>   The lonely Isles of the Sea.'
>
> *Olav's Quest.*

MANY years ago I remember the first time I read that marvellous description of the Maelström by Edgar Allan Poe, where he tells how a fisherman from the Lofoten Islands, driven by a hurricane, was caught in the Maelström's grip, and descended 'into the mouth of that terrific funnel, whose interior, as far as the eye could fathom it, was a smooth, shining, and jet-black wall of water, speeding dizzily round and round with a swaying and sweltering motion, and sending forth to the winds an appalling voice—half-shriek, half-roar—such as not even the mighty cataract of Niagara ever lifts up in its agony to Heaven'; and I remember how I used to picture to myself precipitous, polished cliffs of terrific height and grandeur encircling a writhing pool of dusky waters; above, the rocks glowing red and golden in the light of a stormy sunset; below, stray flakes of foam ever and again flashing back the fiery glories of the angry sky, as they glided with a stealthy, increasing haste for ever nearer and nearer and yet nearer to the awful abyss of the devouring whirlpool. This, like so many tales of one's youth, although told by that consummate artist Poe, must be relegated to the realms of fiction.

But his description of one of the Lofoten Islands—of the 'sheer, unobstructed precipices of black, shining rock,' against which the ocean surf howled and shrieked, and of the endless array of gloomy mountains, 'outstretched like ramparts of the world, hideously craggy and barren'—is far nearer the truth; for in it is much that is characteristic of the outer islands. But after all he has only portrayed the Lofoten Islands when enveloped in storm. Of course, when the south-west gales sweep on to the rock-bound coast of Röst and Moskenesö, even Poe himself could hardly do justice to the scene, for the battle between the great waves coming in from the open ocean and the tremendous tides that surge past the outer islands must be magnificent. Truly the picture would have to be of

> 'An iron coast and angry waves,
> You seemed to hear them rise and fall
> And roar rock-thwarted under bellowing caves,
> Beneath the windy wall.'

Lofoten

But these mere rude phases of Nature's moods do not for ever encircle Lofoten in flying surf and with winds that shriek and howl. In the summer months, at least, the sun shines, and often one may look in vain over the untroubled water, rippled by the warm west wind, for the dreaded Maelström, whose thunderous voice and angry whirlpool for the moment is stilled; whilst in its stead a gentle murmur rises from the clear water which possesses just sufficient motion for the waves to lazily rise and fall against the bare rocky shore, and yet is calm enough for the reflection of the white clouds and craggy hill-sides to repose sleepily on its surface. From their geographical position these islands should have a very different climate from that which they possess; and perhaps it may be due partly to this cause that the mountains are so craggy and barren. For the rainfall during several months is excessive, and is quite capable of washing away any superincumbent earth from the sides of the numerous needle-shaped peaks that are to be found on most of the Lofoten Islands; moreover, in the valleys the whole country has been worn down to the bone in prehistoric times by enormous glaciers, and to-day the abnormal summer rainfall and the frosts of the long Arctic nights are continuing the work of denudation.

Although the Lofoten Islands are south of the North Cape, yet one does not at once appreciate how far north they lie. From London they are more than twelve hundred miles; and they are one hundred miles nearer the North Pole than the northernmost part of Iceland. Moreover, most of Siberia, Bering Straits, and Klondike are all further south than the Lofoten Islands.

If it were not for that warm current which, starting from the Gulf of Mexico, after thousands of miles sweeps past this northern coast of Norway, these islands would during the whole year be covered with ice and snow, and be surrounded by a frozen ocean.

The influence of the Gulf Stream on the temperature of the northern coast of Norway is well illustrated by the fact that every winter the sea round the Lofoten Islands, and even further north at Hammerfest and the North Cape, is always open; yet in Southern Norway, six hundred miles to the southward, the Kristiania Fjord, which the Gulf Stream does not touch, is during the winter months covered with ice. The exact reverse in climate is experienced in Newfoundland, the shores of which are washed by the Labrador current, coming from the frozen north out of Baffin Bay. In the straits of Belle Isle, which are in the same latitude as London, and which separate Newfoundland from Labrador, may be seen snow-drifts on the seashore even in July, whilst the bare uplands behind are covered with far-stretching fields of snow.

The icebergs, too, which drift south on this Labrador current, are sometimes found in such low latitudes that if on the map the latitude were followed due east it would be found to pass through Cairo, and not many miles north of Lahore in India. The approach to the Lofoten Islands from the south after one has passed the Arctic Circle is particularly grand and beautiful. The mountains, owing to excessive prehistoric glaciation, possess forms at once curious and peculiar, giving an individuality to the view which is lacking further south on the Norwegian coast. Lofoten, however, is not seen till the great West Fjord is reached; then far away across thirty miles of blue waters, which slowly pulsate with the long waves of the open sea, appears a wonderful land of sharp-pointed peaks that with a deep sapphire colour outshines the deeper purple of the restless sea.

The west coast of Scotland can give similar views. Rum, Skye, and the Hebrides, as seen from the mainland at Arisaig or Loch Maree, in some respects resemble these islands, but the Lofoten mountains are far wilder and far more fantastic in shape, and the number of peaks infinitely greater than in the western islands of Scotland.

Ages ago the West Fjord must have held an enormous glacier, although it is improbable that the great ice-sheet which then covered the country ever was thick enough to submerge the loftier summits of the Lofoten Islands, the highest of which now stand 4000 feet above sea-level; yet this ice-sheet must have been thousands of feet thick, for from any mountain-top it is easy to see how whole masses of solid rock appear to have been cut away, leaving valleys whose cross-section is a perfect half-circle. To those who are sceptical of what ice will do, a visit to the mainland opposite the Lofoten Islands would prove very instructive.

Even the most gigantic of Himalayan glaciers are feeble in comparison with an Arctic ice-sheet such as that on Greenland or on the Antarctic continent. On Nanga Parbat I have seen a vast glacier turned to one side by its own moraine. Near Elvegaard on the Ofoten Fjord there exist valleys whose sides for miles are perpendicular walls of rock sometimes a couple of thousand feet high, and which undoubtedly have been excavated and then polished by the power of the ice.

For many years I had been anxious to see the

Lofoten Islands, for I had heard rumours that they were more beautiful than Skye and the Coolin. But it was not till 1901 that I was able to go there. It was in good company that I went; Woolley, Hastings, and Priestman, all of whom had been there before in 1897, were the other members of the party. They were able to advise where to go, how to best overcome the difficulties of provisioning our camp, and, what was still better, were all able to speak Norsk fluently.

We landed from the steamer at Svolvaer, a curious harbour amongst a maze of ice-polished rocks. Svolvaer is the point where all the large steamers call, although on a rough day as the vessel approaches the harbour it looks as if there was not even a passage for a rowing-boat anywhere along the rock-bound shore. The small town of Svolvaer is built on a series of rocky islands, consequently the only convenient way of getting from one part of the town to another is by boat, and of course there is no such thing as a road in the town.

The finest mountains in the Lofoten Islands congregate round the Raftsund, a narrow waterway which separates the islands of Hindö and Öst Vaagö; but further down the islands are other isolated peaks whose pointed spires of rock look almost inaccessible. Vaage Kallen is one, whilst several in Moskenesö also would give excellent climbing. As far as I could see, these mountains to the south-west are without glaciers, which is not the case of those round the Raftsund.

The highest peak in Lofoten, Mösadlen by name, had been climbed, but the next three highest, Higraf Tind, 3780 feet; Gjeitgaljar, 3560 feet; and Rulten, 3490 feet, had as yet summits untrodden by the foot of man. Moreover, of all the lesser mountains only about half a dozen had been ascended. Here, then, should the climbing be good, was a mountaineer's paradise.

On August 2, with the help of two men and a couple of boats, Woolley, Hastings, Priestman, and I conveyed our camp-baggage from Svolvaer to a spot marked Austavindnes near the head of the Östnes Fjord. A Norwegian porter, E. Hogrenning, who had been with Hastings before on the mountains for more than one season, also came and helped to pull the heavily laden boats through the waves of the fjord. It was a pleasing sight to me as I sat idle in the stern of the boat in which were the two local fishermen, to watch Hastings and Priestman in their shirt-sleeves pulling the second boat, and trying their best to show that Englishmen were just as capable of rowing as

Norwegians. In this they were successful, for we soon parted company, Hastings' boat finally disappearing on the opposite side of the fjord. In time, however, they came back again to us, but what they had been doing was not quite clear—Hastings had probably been trying to borrow something from a house on the shore, a pole or a cooking-stove, or some nails or a spade. All these things and many more were ultimately collected by Hastings, and before we left our camp a fortnight later there were few houses on the Östnes Fjord that had not contributed something towards our wants. Hastings' tent in the meantime had assumed the appearance of a really first-class gipsy encampment.

The place where we had decided to camp was finally reached, and all our provisions, tents, and baggage landed on the beach. One of the boats we kept, and our two fishermen, bidding us farewell, returned to Svolvaer.

The views from our camp, although rather restricted, were occasionally most beautiful, when during the long summer nights the peaks at the head of the Östnes Fjord to the north-west were a dark purple against the evening sky. Opposite to us was the peak Gjeitgaljar, a veritable little Dru in appearance, and in front of it a ridge of pinnacles that looked hopelessly inaccessible.

Every few moments some change in light and shade or in colour would shift over the landscape. As soon as we had got our camp into order, Woolley and I determined to start the attack on the mountains at once. As far as we knew, all the peaks on the east side of the fjord were unclimbed. We were not joined by Hastings and Priestman, they having to return to Svolvaer for some more baggage. Straight behind our camp the hill-side rose sheer; up these precipitous slabs of glacier-worn rock we made our way, using the small ledges on which grew grass and moss. So steep was the mountain-side that when a spot was reached fully a thousand feet above our camp, it looked as if we could almost have thrown a stone on to the white tents below by the water's edge.

After that we came to more easy travelling, still, however, over glaciated rocks, finally reaching a small glacier.

All along the head of the glacier were precipitous rocks, rising here and there to peaks forming the watershed of the island. At the head and towards the right lay a snow col, filling a deep gap in the rock wall in front of us. Towards this we made our way. The ascent of the ridge from this col to the left was by no means easy climbing, and we soon found that ridge-climbing in the Lofoten, even though there was no ice on the rocks, was often difficult and sometimes impossible. Eventually, by a series of traverses on the south-east side and by climbing up some cracks, we succeeded in reaching our first summit. Here a cairn was built, and I photographed an exceedingly tame ptarmigan in the foreground against an excessively savage-looking peak in the background named Rulten. We were at a height of about 3000 feet. Rulten, from where we were, looked hopelessly inaccessible; but Higraf Tind, the second highest peak in Lofoten, when examined through a glass, promised not only a fine climb, but also success.

One of the great charms of climbing in Lofoten is that to hurry is unnecessary, for it is daylight through all the twenty-four hours: a night out on the mountains in darkness is impossible. Moreover, owing to the comparative smallness of the mountains more than one first ascent may be made in a morning or an afternoon.

As Woolley and I saw several more summits on our ridge (the Langstrandtinder) towards the north-east, we started off for them after we had fully exhausted the view, and smoked as many pipes as were necessary to produce a sensation of rest. In fact, to me one of the chief reasons for moving on to the next peak was that again I might have the excuse for being lazy, again look at the sky, the far-off mountains, and the endless expanse of the sea beyond. The climbing along the ridge was easy, and two more summits were ascended; a small cairn was left on each of their tops.

Further progress along the ridge was, however, impossible, for a deep gap of about five hundred feet cut us off from the next peak. We therefore descended on the north side of the mountain to a steep snow slope, which led down for several hundreds of feet to the glacier below. Thence following our route of the morning we descended the steep rock face above our camp, and got home in time for dinner.

During the next two days we paid a part of our penalty for being on the shores of the Gulf Stream. Clouds hid the mountains, and rain and dull weather kept us at sea-level. But magnificent weather followed on August 7, and we were all impatient to start for the virgin peak, Higraf Tind, 3780 feet, the second highest mountain in Lofoten.

In order to get to the base of the mountain we rowed in our boat across the small arm of the Östnes Fjord, by whose shores we were camped, and beached our boat at Liland. Thence making our way through the thickets of dwarf birch up the lower stretches of the small valley of Lilandsdal, we arrived at the foot of the great precipice which constitutes the upper part of the mountain.

Rimming the head of the valley was the rocky ridge which connects Higraf Tind with Gjeitgaljar. To follow this ridge to the summit of our mountain would have necessitated climbing over various pinnacles and notches, and as we were very sceptical as to whether we should be able to surmount these difficulties, we turned to our left along a small ledge which appeared to run in and out of the gullies that seamed this southern face of Higraf Tind.

On more than one occasion we found ourselves in places where great care was necessary, and our spirits rose and fell as we either found a narrow ledge which would safely lead us into one of the many rock gullies and out again on the far side, or were forced back to try higher up or lower down on the face of the mountain.

Eventually we emerged on the arête which led up to the topmost peak. The summit of the mountain consisted of huge monoliths of what I should call granite (it may, however, be gabbro), similar in appearance to those on the top of the Charmoz, and also similar to the Charmoz in being very narrow with tremendous precipices on each side.

A short distance below the top a small promontory on the ridge afforded a splendid point from which a photograph could be taken. Woolley was sent on so that he might be photographed, proudly planting his ice-axe on the topmost pinnacle. In due time he appeared clear cut against the sky; but immediately afterwards from his gesticulations I could see that something was wrong. The reason was obvious when after a few moments I joined him. Twenty feet away was another summit a few feet higher, and between the two a gulf was fixed.

Below us the rock fell sheer for over thirty feet with never a crack in it, whilst on the opposite side of the chasm the great blocks overhung, so that even had we descended hand over hand on the rope into the gap, direct ascent on the other side was hopeless.

But remembering our tactics lower down we tried further back for a traverse, and soon found that by climbing down a crack between two huge blocks on the eastern side we could get round into the gap. So far so good, but how to surmount the difficulties on the further side! An attempt to traverse on the western side was seen to be hopeless, but an obliging ledge on the other face ran round a corner. Where would it lead to? Cautiously we edged along it, passing under the summit of the mountain. Another crack between great slabs was found; up this we clambered, and once at its top all difficulty disappeared. We had conquered Higraf Tind, and all that remained for us to do was to crown the vanquished mountain with a cairn.

Then we returned to the lower summit, where the cameras and baggage had been left. After toil came repose. The afternoon was perfect, only a few clouds floated in the clear sky. Far away to the south-west could be seen the outer Lofoten Islands, a mass of tangled mountain forms, in colour every conceivable shade of atmospheric blue and purple, whilst beyond lay the calm glittering ocean, and far, far away the last and loneliest of the Lofoten, the island of Röst. Nearer and beneath us were numberless peaks, the majority of them unclimbed; of them, next in height to Higraf Tind were Gjeitgaljar and Rulten. In the distance across the Raftsund in the island of Hindö we could see Mösadlen and its two attendant pinnacles of rock. These pinnacles, from their appearance, should be excessively difficult to climb.

At our feet lay the Blaaskovl glacier with the Troldfjordvatn beyond, a solitary iceberg floating on its waters, and further the Trold Fjord and glimpses of the Raftsund. All these combined to give an effect of space and depth to the view far in excess of what one would expect from mountains not 4000 feet above their base.

We lingered for a long time on the summit; but in a land where, at that time of year, night never comes, what need was there to hurry? The extraordinary atmospheric colours, the ever-changing forms of the clouds, and the slowly slanting rays of the sun, flashing first on one peak and then on another, produced a wonderful picture. Also it was the first time that I had been able to master the complicated geography of the district, and the peaks Store Trold Tind, Svartsund Tind, Isvand Tind, and others that my friends had climbed when they were last camped by the Raftsund, were pointed out to me. No icy wind shrilled across the mountains, darkness would not visit this land for many days yet; to hasten would have been as foolish as it was unnecessary.

After our victory over Higraf Tind came the deluge; for three nights and days the heavens were opened and the rains descended. Had it not been for strenuous efforts on our part in trench digging, our camp would have been bodily washed into the fjord. On one morning an aluminium pan out in the open served as an amateur rain-gauge; in three hours about three inches of water were registered, proving that Lofoten can easily compete with our Atlantic coast as regards rainfall.

On the return of fine weather we determined to attack Rulten. In our boat we rowed to his base, landing in a small bay named Flaeskvik. The lower slopes of the mountain were very steep, and the usual climbing from ledge to ledge and up gullies had to be resorted to.

After a toilsome climb, for the day was moist and warm, we finally emerged on to the true south-west arête, having discovered on our way up a most remarkable window in one of the ridges.

The difficulties now began, for the ridge at once steepened; moreover, in slimness it almost resembled the Grépon. I tried to climb straight up the ridge, but perpendicular slabs, with only small cracks in them, barred the way. To be entirely outside the mountain, when in a peculiarly difficult place, is by no means pleasant. The imagination is far less troubled with ideas of what might happen should one fall, when the extreme steepness is partially hidden from one's view in the privacy of a rock chimney.

Baffled in my attempt to make a direct ascent, I looked to the left for some convenient traverse. There was none; vertical slabs, many hundreds of feet high, entirely stopped the way. To the right hand a ledge was found which led for a short distance along the side of the mountain, but smooth rocks, bending over into space, brought my investigations there also to an abrupt conclusion. It might have been possible from the end of this traverse to climb upwards on to the ridge, but later we saw, on our return journey, that should we have surmounted this difficulty, further along the sky-line more than one gap would almost certainly have prevented our reaching the top. The point where we stopped was below 3000 feet, therefore there was at least 800 feet more of the mountain to climb.

Rulten is undeniably a difficult peak; at present I have seen no likely way up it, but no doubt by a systematic attack, by trying first one side and then another, a weak spot would be discovered.

During the day we had seen the Östnes Fjord dotted over with thousands of boats, and as we descended on to the beach, we found many of the fisherfolk on shore drying their herring-nets on the rocks, for it was the herring fishery that had brought them into the fjord.

These nets are often as much as 800 feet long by 100 to 130 feet deep, and a really fortunate haul will bring in often many hundreds of pounds worth of fish; enough, in fact, to fill more than one small steamer.

It is, of course, in the early spring, from January to April, that the great cod fishery is carried on, for it is then that the cod migrate to the coast. The fish are caught with hooks and lines, and it is the cod fishery which forms the chief trade of the Lofoten Islands.

There are two usual methods of preparing the fish for the market, either by drying (Törfisk) or salting (Klipfisk). The former is the old-fashioned method, and is carried out by drying the cod on wooden scaffolds, after they have been cleaned and the heads removed. And an ancient rule forbade fish being hung up after April 12th, or taken down before June 12th. By far the greater portion of the cod, however, are exported as Klipfisk, Spain being the chief customer, taking about three-fifths of the whole amount exported. Of the remainder of the cod, the liver produces cod-liver oil, the roe is exported to France for sardine bait, and the heads and other parts are turned into manure.

The next day was gloriously fine, so we stretched our Alpine ropes to their fullest extent, between the birch trees, and hung everything in the camp on them to dry. Then we bathed in the clear water of the fjord, taking headers into the deep water from the smoothly polished rocks on the shore.

Ever since we had pitched our tents by the side of the fjord, Gjeitgaljar Tind had waited patiently. Day by day we had seen the mists play hide-and-seek behind his jagged pinnacles of rock; now we thought the time had arrived for us to attack this formidable looking aiguille. In appearance by far the most difficult peak we had seen, it turned out the most easy to climb; in fact, there was no difficulty experienced anywhere on the ascent.

Our route lay up a deep gully partly filled with snow, on the left of the peak, which led us on to a small snow-field behind the summit. On the way up this gully a splendid view of the pinnacle ridge, in front of the top of the mountain, was obtained. A more formidable series of rock towers I have never seen. From the snow-field to the highest point is easy climbing. The top consists of some flat slabs of rock, but the eastern edge is most sensational, and is best investigated by lying on one's stomach before looking over, for it drops sheer for many hundreds of feet. A small stone let fall from the outstretched hand is almost out of sight before it hits the vertical side of the mountain.

A more ideal summit for a cairn could hardly be imagined; moreover, there were plenty of loose stones, so Hogrenning was set to build one worthy of the mountain. He produced one seven feet high, and big enough to proclaim to all interested the fact that somebody at least had scaled that impossible looking rock pinnacle Gjeitgaljar.

On the next day we broke up our camp, putting on board the steamer *Röst* all our baggage; but it was not till late on the day following that we arrived back again at Svolvaer, for the *Röst* had to call at all the small hamlets on the outer islands, almost as far down as the end of Moskenesö. We stopped just short of the historic Maelström, but had we gone further the Maelström would not have been seen, for we voyaged through summer seas.

Hastings now left us in order to go to the Lyngen peninsula, whilst Woolley, Priestman, and I went to Digermulen on the Raftsund.

From there, that most extraordinary fjord, the Trold Fjord was visited, and we also walked up to the Troldfjordvatn. This mountain tarn, hidden away amongst the mountains and flanked with dark and forbidding precipices, has a beauty all its own, and in some respects reminds one of Loch Coruisk.

At its head is a small glacier, whose snout, occasionally breaking off, produces icebergs. The precipices along its shore fall sheer into its dark waters, and the surrounding peaks are wild and savage, but its sides lack the wonderful soft-coloured clothing of the heather, and the rocks are not of such rich hues as the gabbro of Skye. Perhaps I may be wrong, yet it seemed to me that the mountains themselves are not so graceful, neither are the long curving lines so fine as those that can be seen amongst the Coolin from the shores of Coruisk.

From Digermulen we attempted the ascent of another of the unclimbed peaks of Öst Vaagö. It is an unnamed peak north of Rörhop Vand. But the weather was bad, and clouds prevented us ever seeing the summit of our peak. We had, however, a most delightful climb, first up a small glacier, marked Dijerna on the map, thence up some steep rocks to the ridge, which joined our mountain with the Troldtinder. Following this ridge, we ultimately got into a gap, but beyond this we could see no possible way; traversing for a short distance on the western face only showed us that there was little likelihood of our ever getting back again on to the arête, so reluctantly we returned, and got back to Digermulen in the rain.

The weather then went from bad to worse. So we boarded the steamer *Röst* once more, and went for a trip in mist, rain, and storm round Langö, one of the outer islands of Vesteraalen. All that we saw were the grey seas, the clouds lying low on the mountains, and most extraordinary places bristling with rocks, into which our captain took the small *Röst*, tossed to and fro by the great rolling waves of the Arctic ocean. The voyage in fine weather must be superb.

On our return to Svolvaer, Woolley and I travelled south with Priestman, as far as Trondhjem, and from there went home to England.

It is a very curious fact that so few mountaineers go to Lofoten. As far back as 1867 the Rev. St. John Tyrwhitt read a paper before the Alpine Club, in which he says, 'An exploration of the Loffodens would be a work worthy of the Club in every sense of the words.' Again, in 1869, Professor Bonney, who visited these islands with E. Walton, speaks 'strongly of the wonderful grandeur and beauty of some parts of the Lofotens,' and then the next paper in the *Alpine Club Journal* is that of Priestman in 1898 nearly thirty years later.

It is true that the peaks are only 4000 feet high, and therefore cannot compete with those of 14,000 feet; also, they possess no large glaciers, neither are the valleys filled with pine forests, and the foregrounds, as a rule, are desolate and the rocks without much colour: but the rock climbing is as good as any one could wish to get, the rock resembling in many respects that of the Chamonix Aiguilles.

Moreover, and herein lies the strong charm of this mountain-land, it is a land of exquisite atmospheric effects. For those who care to climb where great expanses of sky and clouds arch slowly down to the far-off horizon, and where lonely islands are set in open spaces of blue water, these remote Lofoten mountain fastnesses beyond the Arctic Circle are difficult to equal. The low circling sun making it for ever afternoon, flooding sky and mountain-land in warm, luminous colour, which deepens the distances, and adds perspective to ridge after ridge of serrated and barren peaks, all these purely æsthetic qualifications are possessed in a high degree by the Lofoten Islands. Also for those who are willing to spend a lazy, delightful summer holiday in camp by the side of the many-voiced sea, far from busy crowds and the worries of civilisation, there are few spots more peaceful, more fascinating, or more beautiful than these Lofoten Islands, where the wondrous summer skies slowly change their exquisitely rich colouring of long-drawn-out evening for the more delicate tints of the early dawn, and where the restless waves of the great Arctic Ocean are for ever washing against the precipitous sides of the bare, rock-girt mountains.

A CHUILIONN

'But in the prime of the summer-time
Give me the Isle of Skye.'

A. NICOLSON.

ONCE upon a time, as the story-books say, Dr. Samuel Johnson was bold enough to forsake his beloved Fleet Street, and, at the age of sixty-four, journey northwards in company with Boswell to the Hebrides, the Ultima Thule of those days. He finally arrived in the Island of Skye, 'without any memorable accident,' about the beginning of September 1773, where he experienced all the severities of ordinary Skye weather—much rain and many gales—and this state of things continuing throughout the month, the Doctor found some difficulty in getting back again to the mainland. He writes, 'Having been detained by storms many days in Skie, we left, as we thought with a fair wind; but a violent gust which Bos had a great mind to call a tempest, forced us into Col, an obscure island.'

The wild and beautiful scenery of the Island of Skye does not seem to have made any impression on Johnson, and he leaves with no regret, merely admitting, that he has 'many pictures in his mind which he could not have had without his journey,' and that these pictures 'will serve later for pleasing topics of conversation.' What these pictures were he does not say, but they probably had little to do with what we now call the beauties of the Highlands; for he mentions that he found little entertainment in the wildernesses of the Hebrides, the universal barrenness oppressed him, and he points out that 'in those countries you are not to suppose that you shall find villages or enclosures. The traveller wanders through a naked desert, gratified sometimes but rarely with sight of cows, and now and then finds heaps of loose stones and turf in a cavity between the rocks, where a being, born with all those powers which education expands, and all those sensations which culture refines, is condemned to shelter itself from the wind and the rain.' Also, that 'a walk upon ploughed fields in England is a dance upon carpets, compared to the toilsome drudgery of wandering in Skie.' But it is not surprising that Johnson at the age of sixty-four looked upon hilly country with aversion —the mountains interfered with his convenience. He only mentions the hills in Skye once. 'Here are mountains that I should once have climbed,' he writes to his friend Mrs. Thale; 'but to

The Coolin

climb steeps is now very laborious, and to descend them dangerous.' No doubt at the Doctor's age he was right; still we feel somewhat disappointed that during his stay at Talisker, he was apparently unconscious of the Coolin, and we receive but small consolation from his elegant epistolary communications, when they tell us instead, that he was gratified sometimes but rarely with sight of cows, and that Mr. Boswell was affected almost to tears by the illustrious ruins at Iona.

All this shows us, how the attitude of people towards the wilds of the Highlands has become completely changed in one century, for Johnson was not in any way peculiar in his ideas. Look where we will in the literature of that time, we find the same sentiments. Pennant, who visited Skye the year before Dr. Johnson, describes the Coolin as 'a savage series of rude mountains,' whilst Blaven, 'affects him with astonishment.' Thirty years later the only natural objects in the island that interested Forsyth, at least so far as one can judge from what he writes in *The Beauties of Scotland*, were 'an obelisk of uncommon magnitude' in the parish of Snizort, (probably the Storr Rock,) and a waterfall and sea cave near Portree.

But a new school was growing up, and Sir

Walter Scott was one of the first to insist, that a visit to the Highlands would reveal objects more interesting than cows, waterfalls, and sea caves. People were beginning to find in the torrents, mountains, lochs, and pine woods, beauties they had not seen before. No longer were the hills chaotic masses of rock, ready at any moment to fall and overwhelm the valleys, nor were the moors and glens expanses of uniform barrenness or gloomy mountain fastnesses. Robson, at the beginning of last century (1815), writing of one of the most remote and wild regions of the Highlands, namely the head of Glen Tilt, says: 'Of all the romantic scenes which are presented to those who explore the recesses of the Grampians, none will be found to possess a more picturesque combination of wild and characteristic beauty than this'; and in the preface to his accurate and delightful volume on the scenery of the Grampian mountains, he writes: 'With the man of taste few districts in this kingdom have equal claim to admiration.'

Robson was not a Scotchman, but a London artist; yet one has only to look at his sketches, and read the letterpress of his book to see how well he appreciated mountain form, and how he understood, in no uncertain manner, that which now delights us nearly a century later in the Highlands.

His water-colour picture of Loch Coruisk [1] is an honest attempt to accurately reproduce the wonderful colour and savage beauty of the grandest of all Scotch lochs, and one is only sorry that he has introduced into the foreground a fully dressed Highlander—a legacy, no doubt, of that old feeling that made Dr. Johnson crave for cows, and that even now survives at the present time in the pretty sketches of Scotch hills, where the foreground is animated by Highland cattle.

Since Robson's time, many people have been to the Highlands and to Skye and the Coolin. Turner visited them, and the impression produced may be seen from his drawing of Loch Coriskin. This drawing is described by Ruskin in *Modern Painters* as 'a perfect expression of the Inferior Mountains,' yet any one who had really seen the Coolin would hardly be justified in asserting that Turner's drawing (Fig. 69, vol. iv., *Modern Painters*) was the perfect expression of the hills round Sgurr Dubh, even though it may be the perfect expression of an inferior mountain.

Fortunately the Coolin are never inferior mountains, unless we measure them by the number of feet they rise above the sea. 'Comparative bulk and height,' says the late Sheriff Nicolson, 'are of

[1] It used to be in the Loan Collection at the South Kensington Museum.

course important elements in mountain grandeur, but outline and features are, as with human beings, even more important.' Clachlet at Easter, covered with snow and seen across the moor of Rannoch at a distance of a few miles, towers up into the heavens just as grandly as a peak five times its altitude does in the Himalaya, when that peak is seen from a point thirty miles away.

It is the atmosphere that adds both dignity and charm to these Scotch hills, making them appear far bigger than they would in the clearer air of the larger mountain ranges, and giving them all the softened colour and perspective so necessary to emphasise the real beauty of true mountains. Their form also helps them in no small degree. The long-flowing lines of the lower slopes gradually rising from the moorland below, and the beautifully carved corries that nestle into their sides, all tend to strengthen and serve as a fit substructure for their more wild and broken summits.

At their feet lie no valleys with dirty-white glacier streams tearing down between mud banks, and never a proper pool in them; their sides are not disfigured with monotonous pine forests of a uniform light green colour, but the heather and the grey rocks, lichen-covered, mingle together on their slopes, lighting up with every flash of sunshine, or deepening into every shade of brown and purple gloom, as the storm clouds sweep over their summits; whilst, below, brown trout streams wander between wild birches and Scotch firs, staying here in some dark pool hidden away under the rocks covered with ferns and heather, flashing out again there into the sunshine over the pebbles, and across the low-lying moor.

Those who have seen the Coolin from the moors above Talisker in the twilight, or who have watched them on a summer's evening from Kyle Akin, apparently clothed in deep purple velvet broidered with gold, and rising out of the 'wandering fields of barren foam,' whilst

> 'The charmed sunset linger'd low adown
> In the red west';

or lazily spent a whole day on the sand beaches of Arisaig point, gazing, towards Rum and Skye lying light blue on the horizon, and across a sea brilliant in colour as the Mediterranean amongst the Ionian islands; or lingered at the head of Loch Coruisk till the last pale light has faded out of the heavens behind Sgùrr Alasdair, and only the murmur of the streams breaks the stillness of the night air—those who have thus seen the Coolin will know that they are beautiful. But the fascination that these mountains exercise over those that know them well is manifold; there are more pleasures that the Coolin can offer than those of being merely very beautiful. For the mountaineer who wanders in the heart of this marvellous mountain land there are rock climbs without end. He can spend hour after hour exploring the corries, or threading the intricacies of the narrow rock edges that form so large a part of the sky-line. From the summits he can watch the mists sweeping up from below, and hurrying over the bealachs in tumbled masses of vapour, or he can dreamily follow the white sails of the boats, far out to sea, as they slowly make for the outer islands; then clambering down the precipitous faces he can repose in some sheltered nook and listen to the sound of a burn, perhaps a thousand feet below, echoed across from the sheer walls of rock on the other side of the corrie; there is always something new to interest him—it may be a gully that requires the utmost of his skill as a mountaineer, or it may be a view of hill, moor, and loch backed by the Atlantic and the far-off isles of the western sea. Nowhere in the British Islands are there any rock climbs to be compared with those in Skye, measure them by what standard you will—length, variety, or difficulty. Should any one doubt this, let him some fine morning walk up from the head of Coruisk to the rocky slabs at the foot of Sgurr a'Ghreadaidh. There he will see the bare grey rocks rising out from the heather not 500 feet above the level of the loch, and there walls, ridges, and towers of weather-worn gabbro stretch with hardly a break to the summit of the mountain, 2800 feet above him. Measured on the map, it is but half a mile, but that half mile will tax his muscles; he must climb up gullies that the mountain torrents have worn out of the precipices, and over slabs of rock sloping down into space at an angle that makes handhold necessary as well as foothold; he must creep out round edges on to the faces of perpendicular cliffs, only to find that after all the perpendicular cliff itself must be scaled before he can win back again to the ridge that is to lead him to the topmost peak. There are many such climbs in the Coolin. The pinnacles of Sgurr nan Gillean, the four tops of Sgurr a'Mhadaidh, and the ridge from Sgurr Dearg to Sgurr Dubh, are well known, but the face climbs have been neglected. The face of Sgurr a'Mhadaidh from Tairneilear, the face of Sgurr Alasdair from Coire Labain, are both excellent examples of what these mountains can offer to any one who wants a first-rate scramble on perfect rock. Sgurr a'Coir' an Lochain on the northern face gives a climb as good as one could anywhere wish to get, yet it is only a preliminary one to those on the giants Sgurr Alasdair and Sgurr Dearg that lie behind.

But splendid though the climbing on the Coolin may be, it is only one of the attractions, possibly a minor attraction, to these hills, and there are many other mountain ranges where rock-climbing can be found. It is the individuality of the Coolin that makes the lover of the hills come back again and again to Skye, and this is true also of other mountain districts on the mainland of Scotland. To those who can appreciate the beauty of true hill form, the ever-changing colour and wonderful power and character of the sea-girt islands of the west, the lonely grandeur of Rannoch moor, the spacious wooded valley of the Spey at Aviemore, backed by the Cairngorm mountains, wild Glen Affric prodigal of gnarled pines abounding in strange curves of strength, or the savage gloom of Glencoe—all these scenes tell the same tale, and proclaim in no doubtful manner, that the Scotch mountain land in its own way is able to offer some of the most beautiful mountain scenery in the world.

The Highlands of Scotland contain mountain form of the very finest and most subtle kind—form not so much architectural, of which Ruskin writes, 'These great cathedrals of the earth, with their gates of rock, pavements of clouds, choirs of streams and stone, altars of snow, and vaults of purple traversed by the continual stars,' but form where the savage grandeur, the strength, and the vastness of the mountains is subordinate to simpler, yet in a way more complicated, structures. Scotch mountains have something finer to give than architectural form. In their modelling may be seen the same beauties that in perfection exist in Greek statuary. The curving lines of the human figure are more subtle than those of any cathedral ever built. The Aiguilles round Mont Blanc are architectural in the highest degree, but the mighty summit rising up far above them into the blue sky, draped in wonderful and sweeping lines of snow and ice, marvellously strong, yet full of moderation, is far more mysterious, far more beautiful, than all the serrated ridges and peaks that cluster round its base.

It is in the gentleness of ascent in many of the Highland hills, in the restraint and repose of the slopes 'full of slumber,' that we can trace all the finer and more delicate human lines; and it is due to the strength of these lines that the bigger mountains seem to rise without an effort from the moors and smaller hills that surround them. To many people the Cairngorm range is composed of shapeless, flat-topped mountains devoid almost of any character. They do not rise like the Matterhorn in savage grandeur, yet the sculptured sides of Braeriach, seen from Sgoran Dubh Mhor, are in reality far more full of rich and intricate mountain sculpture, than the whole face of the Matterhorn as seen from the Riffel Alp.

The individuality of the Coolin is not seen in their summits, which are often almost ugly, but in the colour of the rocks, the atmospheric effects, the relative largeness and harmony of the details compared with the actual size of the mountains, and most of all in the mountain mystery that wraps them round: not the mystery of clearness such as is seen in the Alps and Himalaya, where range after range recedes into the infinite distance, till the white snow peaks cannot be distinguished from the clouds, but in the secret beauty born of the mists, the rain, and the sunshine, in a quiet and untroubled land, no longer vexed by the more rude and violent manifestations of the active powers of Nature. Once there was a time when these peaks were the centre of a great cataclysm; they are the shattered remains of a vast volcano that ages since poured its lavas in mighty flood far and wide over the land; since then the glaciers in prehistoric times have polished and worn down the corries and the valley floors, leaving scars and wounds everywhere as a testimony of this power; but the fire age and the ice age are past; now the still, clear waters of Coruisk ripple in the breeze, by the loch-side lie the fallen masses of the hills, and the shattered debris left by the glaciers of bygone days; these harbour the dwarf hazel, the purple heather, and the wildflowers, whilst corrie, glen, and mountain-side bask in the summer sunlight.

But when the wild Atlantic storms sweep across the mountains; when the streams gather in volume, and the bare rock faces are streaked with the foam of a thousand waterfalls; when the wind shrieks amongst the rock pinnacles, and sky, loch, and hill-side all are one dull grey, the Coolin can be savage and dreary indeed. Perhaps, though, the clouds towards evening may break; then the torn masses of vapour tearing in mad hunt along the ridges will be lit up by the rays of the sun slowly descending into the western sea, 'robing the gloom with a vesture of divers colours, of which the threads are purple and scarlet, and the embroideries flame'; and as the light flashes from the black rocks, and the shadows deepen in the corries, the superb beauty, the melancholy, the mystery of these mountains of the Isle of Mist will be revealed. But the golden glory of the sunset will melt from off the mountains, the light that silvered the great slabs will slowly fail; from out the corries darkness heralding the black night will creep with stealthy tread, hiding all in gloom; then, last of all, beyond the darkly luminous, jagged, and fantastic outline of the Coolin the glittering stars will flash from the clear sky, no wind will stir the great quiet, and only the far-off sound, born of the rhythmic murmur of the sea-waves beating on the rock-bound shore of lonely Scavaig, remains as a memory of the storm.

THE MOUNTAINS OF IRELAND

In conclusion, let us sum up the lessons that the mountains of the British Isles can teach us. They can give healthy exercise, and cultivate in us the power of appreciating the beauties and grandeur of nature. . . . Amongst them we may learn the proper uses of our legs. . . . We may learn to climb difficult rocks, to avoid dislodging loose stones, and to guard against those dangers that are peculiar to grassy mountains. . . . We can cultivate perseverance, courage, the quiet, uncomplaining endurance of hardships, and last, but not least important, those habits of constant care and prudence without which mountaineering ceases to be one of the finest sports in the world, and may degenerate into a gambling transaction with the forces of nature, with human life for the stake.'

CHARLES PILKINGTON.

TURNING over the pages one day of the index of the *Alpine Club Journal*, I looked for information on the mountains of Ireland. Greece, Greenland, Patagonia, the Peepsa fly, and mountain midgets were all mentioned, but Ireland and its many ranges of hills I sought for in vain. This obviously was a most monstrous injustice, and it almost seemed, at first sight, as if a tour of exploration into this apparently unknown land might be undertaken for the purpose of climbing the numerous and neglected heights. Years ago, however, I had visited several parts of Ireland, the Mourne mountains, the north of Antrim, and a great part of Donegal, and I knew that there were cairns at least on the summits of most of the mountains; presumably, therefore, they had been visited by man before my arrival.

Still it is strange that Ireland, with so many groups of hills, and some of them so wonderfully beautiful, should not attract more notice in the mountaineering world. Why should not an Irish club, like the Climbers' Club, the Cairngorm Club, or the Scottish Mountaineering Club, be formed? Mr. H. C. Hart, in his introduction to Ireland in *Climbing in the British Isles*, has very ably given both the possibilities and the limits of Irish climbing, and I cannot do better than quote his words: 'But there are ample opportunities for acquiring the art of mountain craft, the instinct which enables the pedestrian to guide himself alone from crest to crest, from ridge to ridge, with the least labour. He will learn how to plan out his course from the base of cliff or gully, marking each foot and hand grip with calm attention; and knowing when to cease to attempt impossibilities, he will learn to trust in himself, and acquire that most necessary of all climbers' acquirements, a philosophic, contemplative calm in the presence of danger or difficult dilemmas. If the beginner is desirous of rock practice, or the practised hand requires to test his

The Macgillicuddy's Reeks.

condition or improve his form, there is many a rocky coast where the muscles and nerves and stamina can be trained to perfection. Kerry and Donegal are competent to form a skilled mountaineer out of any capable aspirant. Ice and snow craft is an accomplishment which must of course be learnt elsewhere.'

All this being true, it seems incomprehensible that Ireland should not be looked upon more favourably as a possible mountaineering country. I am afraid nowadays, however, that unless a considerable amount of rock gymnastics can be made part of a climb, the modern mountaineer is not satisfied. Merely beautiful scenery is insufficient to lure him to the mountains. Still, as Mr. Hart says, Kerry and Donegal are good training-grounds for the novice. This I can vouch for; the cliffs of Slieve League, 1972 feet, form one of the finest sea cliffs in the British Isles, and much of the best scenery amongst the Macgillicuddy's Reeks can only be obtained by those who are willing to do some rock scrambling.

Now the modern mountaineer, owing to this specialisation in rock climbing, is apt to lose much that the earlier mountain climbers enjoyed; whilst, in days gone by, the wanderer amongst the mountains also missed much by being unable to deal with difficult rocks. On the other hand, the expert of to-day gains in both directions, but he must beware of spending all his time in mere gymnastics or the pure athletics of mountaineering. One of Ireland's most famous literary men, the Rev. J. P. Mahaffy, more than a quarter of a century ago in *Social Life in Greece*, points out the dangers of immoderate specialisation in bodily exercise, and how alien it was to Greek education. 'The theoretical educators,' he says, 'knew quite well what most of us do not, that field sports are vastly superior to pure athletics in their effects upon the mind.' Again: 'The Greeks knew what we ignore, that such sports as require excessive bodily training and care are low and debasing in comparison to those which demand only the ordinary strength and quickness, daring and decision in danger, resource and ingenuity in difficulties.' In these days the old Greek virtue of moderation is hard to follow. But perhaps in the sport of mountaineering it is more easily observed than in many others, for he who wanders amongst the hills is not driven forward by strenuous competition, no crowd applauds the success of some daring feat, and as a rule these immoderate efforts can be avoided.

The extent of wild mountainous country in

Ireland where the mountaineer can enjoy his sport is much greater than is generally supposed; the Kerry mountains occupy a larger area than the Snowdon group in North Wales; then there are the Wicklow mountains, the Mourne mountains, the Donegal Highlands, the Galtee More group, and the mountainous country of Connemara and Mayo, which last is about forty miles long by thirty miles wide.

Over all these scattered groups the mountaineer can wander at his will; he will be stopped by no one. Moreover, this west coast of Ireland has more to offer than mountains. Should the visitor not be extraordinarily enthusiastic and wish to walk over the hills every day in the week, from Kerry to Donegal there are always plenty of rivers and lakes where salmon and trout can be caught; the scenery, too, is often of the finest description, wonderfully wild sea lochs to explore, with a magnificent rock-bound coast, on whose shores the restless Atlantic breaks, also numberless lonely islands far out in the sea. To those who care for beautiful soft atmospheric lights, for great stretches of heather lands, of sky, or of clouds, for a clean sea with often miles of yellow sands or splendid cliffs, all these can be found on Ireland's Atlantic coast, and they surely are a sufficient enticement to bring far more visitors to this beautiful country than are to be found there at the present time.

It is now many years since I was stopping at Carrick in Donegal bay. Not many miles west of Carrick is Slieve League. Although it is not quite 2000 feet high, yet it needs a good climber to ascend this hill from the seashore at its feet. I do not know what the average angle may be, but on one summer afternoon it took me a very long time to accomplish the ascent.

Of course there is a great deal of heather and grass set at the steepest angle on which they will grow; but a climber ought to be able to be as safe on such a mountain-side as he is on hard rock or on snow or ice, and unless experience is obtained, he will remain a novice in this particular kind of climbing.

There was more than one place on the way up Slieve League from the seashore that needed considerable care, and I well remember those 'nasty ravines, iron-floored and steep-edged,' that Mr. Hart mentions in his description of the place.

Another unique experience, not however a mountaineering one, that I had whilst stopping at Carrick, was in the sea caves in the cliffs just west of Slieve League. It is only in the finest weather that a boat can venture near them, for even after several days of east wind off the land the Atlantic swell is still big enough, unless great care is taken, to break a rowing boat to pieces on the rocks.

The cliffs where the cave is situated come down sheer into the dark water below; the entrance is a great doorway with a somewhat slanting roof, into which the full force of the waves from the open ocean can play; and as the boat rises and falls on the water, the danger of hidden rocks underneath the surface adds a certain amount of anxiety to the other feelings that possess one, as the daylight begins to fade away in the mysterious recesses of the cavern.

For about three hundred yards this tunnel is straight; by looking back the opening can be seen growing smaller and smaller and more distant. At length a great dome-shaped chamber is reached, from which branch out other caves in various directions. Here the dim light of candles, the washing of the water on the rocks, the thunderous booming of the surge in unknown passages far away in the bowels of the mountain, where, every sound being greatly magnified and echoed backwards and forwards, all these produce most weird and awe-inspiring sensations. The mystery and the sense of remoteness from the world, the uncanny feeling that a thousand feet of solid rock lies between one and the sunshine, also add to the effect. But when besides these things, we had been listening to dreadful tales from our boatmen, of mermaids, of sea pigs light green in colour with pink spots and human heads, that at night would come 'wondering' round the boat, and finally of a 'great big beast, a serpent,' as large as the steeple of a church, which was supposed not only to feed on human beings when opportunity offered, but what was worse, was said to inhabit the inner recesses of the very cave in which we were, it is unnecessary to say how easy it was to be frightened at anything.

The only unblocked waterway where a boat could pass on out of this domed hall was to the right, and up this we were preparing to go in search of seal, when some exceptionally large waves, tortured in some narrow passages, sent a terrific boom with multitudinous echoes reverberating through the caverns; at the same time a most curious phenomenon, half sound, half vibration of the air occurred. It seemed as though the whole body of the air in the cave pulsated, producing a swishing sound with periods of about one second, which gradually became fainter and fainter till it died away. Probably the cave had been converted into a gigantic organ pipe, and the note was one so low down in the scale that the vibrations were about one per second.

Unfortunately I suggested that it was the 'great big beast, the serpent,' and that finished the expedition. Our boatmen were at once terrified, shouting to each other, pushing and half rowing the boat in a frenzy of fear. Amidst the bellowing noises of the various caverns leading out of the central hall, and the angry hisses of 'the beast, the serpent,' we departed most hurriedly for the outer air.

Slieve League, however, if the Ordnance Survey maps are to be trusted, is not the finest cliff in Ireland. On the western coast of Achill Island are the cliffs of Croaghaun, 2192 feet high. But my friend, Colin Phillip, who was there in the summer of 1901, made a somewhat startling discovery. A piece of land to the west of Croaghaun, more than *a square quarter of a mile*, has been left out altogether from the map. Where this land should be a bay is marked; perhaps, however, his own words will describe better how the discovery was made. 'The seaward face of Croaghaun is usually spoken of as an almost perpendicular cliff of over 2000 feet. This is not true. It is a fine, rocky, more or less buttressed mountain face, dropping to the sea at an angle of perhaps 50 degrees in places. But its general inclination would not be so much. There appears to be a curious error in the Ordnance Survey map with regard to the sea front of this hill. Expecting to find a grand view of this giant amongst the cliffs of Ireland, I made for a point marked on the map as a headland, projecting well out to sea on the west side of Croaghaun, from which a complete survey of the face should have been obtained. I was astonished to find, instead of a broad bay, with the great cliff of the mountain descending into it, a narrow inlet, like a 'geo' in Shetland, on the other side of which, almost completely blocking the view, was the south-west buttress of Croaghaun, and certainly not steeper than 40 degrees.' The whole bay, therefore, as marked on the Ordnance map, is now occupied by the lower part of the mountain; consequently, instead of a sheer cliff, this western side of the mountain is no more than an easy slope which may be traversed in many places.

Another piece of information of Phillip's which may be novel, is that perhaps Sir Walter Scott was right when he called the hills in Skye the Cuchullin hills. During a discussion on the Skye hills with Mr. Seaton F. Milligan (past vice-president of the Royal Society of Antiquaries of Ireland), whom Phillip met on the west coast of Ireland, Mr. Milligan said that the hills had been named after the Irish hero Cuchulain; and the reason he gave was the following:—

In those early days the sons of the kings of Ireland were often sent to Skye to learn the art of war. At the end of their first year, a test of their progress was whether they were able to walk across what was called 'the bridge of the cliffs'; this bridge is supposed to have been part of the ridge of the Coolin. The bridge is thus described in the legend:—

'Wonderful was the sight the bridge afforded, when any one would leap upon it, for it narrowed until it became as narrow as the hair of one's head, the second time it shortened till it became short as an inch, and the third time it grew slippery until it was as slippery as an eel of the river, and the fourth time it rose up on high against you as the mast of a ship.'

That this description agrees with the ridges of Sgurr nan Gillean (the peak of the young men) no one can deny, and the story goes on to say how Cuchulain at once performs the feat at the first trial, so astonishing the onlookers that the bridge was named after him.

In opposition, however, to this, we have the weighty statement of the late Alexander Nicolson, who says,[1] 'They are known to the natives of Skye and always have been as "A Chuilionn." There was an Ossianic hero of the name Cuchulain, said

[1] *The Scottish Mountaineering Club Journal*, vol. ii. p. 99.

to have been brought up at Dun-Sgàthaich, an ancient fort near Ord in Skye, but the natives never called the great mountain range by his name. In this view I am supported by our greatest Celtic archæologist, Dr. Skene.'

But to return to Ireland: besides the cliffs on Achill, all along the north coast of Mayo are excessively wild and grand precipices often of hard quartzite rock, and this part of the west coast is perhaps the finest and most picturesque in all Ireland.

East and south of Achill lie a series of detached mountains and ranges of mountains, all of which are more or less interesting as they command wide views of sea, valley, and moorland. South of the Killary lies perhaps the most beautiful of all the mountainous districts in Ireland, the district of Connemara. In fact, it is not exaggeration to say that there are few finer groups of hills in Britain than the twelve Bens of Connemara, and this is the more remarkable when one considers that they are only 2395 feet high. To again quote Phillip: 'The views from some of the summits are enchanting, in particular from the easily got at summit W.S.W. of Leenane. From this point the Killary can be traced from the ocean to its head. The valley of the Erriff river carries the eye over the plains of Mayo northwards to the far away hills in Sligo. To the eastward the Formnamore mountains, with glimpses through their gaps of Loughs Maske and Corrib, beyond which the plains extend through Mayo, Galway, to Clare. Then Maam Turk blocks the view, which opens again, however, to the south, with wild moorland and the whole of the twelve Bens. Through the gaps of these mountains the Atlantic is seen in more than one direction, fringed by rocky headlands and white sandy bays, carrying the eye back again to the westward and the solemn Killary, beyond which, lying almost hidden amongst the hills, is the beautiful valley of Delphi and glimpses of the Dhu Lough.'

I have left the Kerry hills till the last, because they are the most important and the highest in Ireland. The Connemara hills are perhaps, on the whole, more beautiful, but the hills of Kerry possess a grandeur and such characteristic form, that one at once thinks of them as mountains and not hills. This is not surprising, for they easily surpass the English hills in height, Carran Tuohill, 3414 feet, Been Keragh, 3314 feet, Caher, 3200 feet, and Brandon, 3127 feet, being the highest.

Moreover their bases are in some cases (Brandon,

for instance) on the seashore. The chief points of this group, which in some respects differentiate them from the other ranges of mountains in the British Isles, are the numberless wild mountain tarns that lie hidden in their corries, the masses of vegetation that clothe even the rock precipices, and the curious capping of peat that is to be found on some of the hill-tops.

In some instances, after climbing up hundreds of feet of rock from the corrie below, one finds that the last twenty feet of the mountain is up a steep slope of peat, occasionally almost corniced by the overhanging fringe of heather. Then, too, the luxuriant growth of the trees in some of the valleys, especially those near Killarney and at the head of Caragh lake, is wonderful, and it is almost needless to say that the upper part of the Lake of Killarney itself, beneath the Macgillicuddy's Reeks, is unrivalled in the British Isles for rich beauty. There are larger lakes surrounded by far wilder scenery in Scotland, for instance in Glen Affric, or lakes like Loch Katrine that lie between wonderful forested shores and beneath shapely mountains, or Rydal Water or parts of Derwentwater in the Lake District; but the upper lake at Killarney, as an example of winding stretches of clear waters, with rocky shores clothed in oaks, firs, hollies, and other trees, the foliage stretching upwards to the heather-covered mountains behind, this particular part of the Kerry mountain land certainly in its own way stands alone; it has no competitor.

The warm moist Atlantic climate has had almost the effect of a hothouse on the flora of these sheltered valleys, whilst above, on the summits of the mountains the first snow and storms of the winter and early spring produce a rugged wildness that is only to be found in the British Islands on mountains over 3000 feet high.

Carran Tuohill, the highest of the Macgillicuddy's Reeks, also the highest mountain in Ireland, lies some distance away from Killarney. Its eastern and northern faces are especially grand. At its foot can be found more than one mountain tarn; Lough Gouragh, at the head of the Hag's Glen, being very fine, for the greatest mountain precipice in Ireland rises from its shores almost to the summit of Carran Tuohill, about 2300 feet above. On the other side of the mountain, another tarn, Coomloughra, is of a more ordinary type, even although it is encircled by the three highest peaks in Ireland. Notwithstanding that the face of Caher, which overlooks Coomloughra, is precipitous for more than 1000 feet, yet there is no very good climbing to be obtained on it, for the rocks are treacherous; also, they run diagonally up and across the face of the mountain.

The views from all these mountains that surround Coomloughra are very fine. That from Been Keragh perhaps is the best for the surrounding peaks; for, looking across the Hag's Glen at the black precipices of Carran Tuohill and at the savage ridge which connects it with Been Keragh, one wonders that such wild and desolate scenery can exist so near to the rich and luxuriant vegetation of the valleys only a few miles away.

From Carran Tuohill it is towards the west and south-west that the finest outlook is obtained. Across the valley in which Coomloughra lies are the cliffs of Caher; Dursey Island is seen in the distance at the mouth of the Kenmare river; the small but shapely Skellig rocks jut out of the open sea far away in the west; and Brandon, one of the most beautiful of mountains, stands alone and solitary on the shores of the wild Atlantic beyond the blue waters and the yellow sands of Dingle bay. Heather moorland, desolate loughs, and peat mosses extend for miles, and the great dome of the sky, perhaps flecked with soft clouds, bends down to the far off horizon of the outer ocean.

To the west of the Macgillicuddy's Reeks, in a part of the country but little visited, is Lough Coomacullen, one of the most wonderfully beautiful mountain tarns I have ever seen. Hidden away amongst the hills, and difficult of access, it has attracted but little attention, yet with its glacier-worn sides of bare rock that descend in many places sheer into the black waters below, and the circle of cliffs which surround the upper part of the lough, one might almost imagine one was in Norway, except that the deep velvet brown of the heather, the few well-grown hollies clinging to the broken rock walls, and the rich colours of the mosses, lichens, and ferns that find nourishment on the ledges and faces of the precipices, at once show that one is on the Atlantic coast and in a softer and warmer clime.

Five hundred feet below this small tarn lies the larger lake, Coomasaharn; it too has a shore line much wilder and more rugged than the majority of British lakes. Great boulders and masses of glacier-worn rocks surround it, whilst at its head the precipices extend almost to the summit of Coomacarrea (2542 feet). In some places these precipices give good rock scrambling, but it is rather surprising, after a couple of hours' climbing on good hard rock, to find that the top of the mountain is a flat peat moor which in some places almost overhangs the wild corrie below.

This capping of peat on several of even the wilder mountains seems to be characteristic of many of the summits on the west coast of Ireland. The highest summits of the Reeks, however, are quite free from peat.

There are, of course, many other mountainous districts besides those I have already mentioned. The Mourne mountains, where the mountaineer may, if he chooses, collect topaz and beryls of a most exquisite blue, the Wicklow, Tipperary, or Waterford groups, all possess wild mountain scenery, and many rare plants can be found there. But after all, undoubtedly it is the picturesque side of the mountain land that makes to the wanderer in Ireland the most forcible appeal of all. It is the atmospheric softness, and the rich vegetation, which, on the west of Ireland, covers the valleys, glens, and the mountain-sides, it is the colour of the deep and lovely tarns, of the expanses of heather, and of the distances, and lastly, it is the rugged, rock-bound coast, a coast of many bays, of desolate islands, of solitary sea stacks, of cliffs, of sandy beaches, and wonderful sea caves, a coast that has for ages withstood the attacks of the mighty waves of the storm-driven Atlantic; these are the beauties of which this Irish mountain land can boast, which after all are of more worth than the attractions of many inaccessible pinnacles and many ranges of ugly but excessively steep and high mountains.

PREHISTORIC CLIMBING NEAR WASTDALE HEAD

> 'Though sluggards deem it but a foolish chase,
> And marvel men should quit their easy chair,
> The toilsome way, and long, long league to trace,
> Oh, there is sweetness in the mountain air
> And life, that bloated Ease can never hope to share.'
>
> *Childe Harold.*

To the mountaineer who makes his way from Seascale or from Drigg to Wastdale Head, the Cumberland hills with their long, rolling outlines, their flanks concealed by superincumbent soil and vegetation, do not seem to promise well as far as rock climbing is concerned. Only here and there do the ridges break into rocky precipices; nowhere is seen the rugged grandeur of the Highlands of Scotland; such valleys as Glencoe with its rock-built walls, or the splintered summits of the Coolin, or of An Teallach, do not exist. Yet the rock-climber who stops at the inn at the head of Wastdale may spend weeks before he has exhausted the district. He will be lucky indeed, and a first-rate climber to boot, if he has done the best of the climbs without further aid than that afforded by what the mountaineer calls the 'moral' support of the rope. Once upon a time a celebrated climber of Alpine repute came to Wastdale for the first, alas! also for the last time. 'Climbing in the Caucasus,' Mummery said, 'was easy and safe; in the Alps too it was usually easy and safe, though sometimes difficult; but climbing as practised at Wastdale Head was both difficult and dangerous.'

The great delight of the climber in the Cumberland hills is in gullies or 'ghylls,' and no wonder, for there are endless gullies both great and small, the climbs in which vary with the state of the weather, and may be easy or difficult, wet or dry, or dirty, according to circumstances. Then again, the climber must have a perfect contempt for streams, and especially waterfalls, for the ascent of a perpendicular 'pitch' through a delightfully cold and invigorating shower bath will be one of his earliest experiences. But there are plenty of other climbs besides those in ghylls. Hidden away in the recesses of the hills are sharp and jagged pinnacles of hard porphyritic rock, precipices smooth, flawless, and sometimes overhanging, whose firm grey bastions have withstood the storms of ages; whilst only at their feet, where lie the remnants which have yielded, flake by flake, from the massive buttresses above, does the ruin proclaim that the hand of time carves the rocks on the mountain-side as well as the valleys below.

This was written several years ago, before all the rock problems, and also before all their variations, had been worked out. When first I visited Wastdale Head it was at Christmas time. I knew there was a pinnacle of rock on Great Gable, also that another rock climb could be obtained on the Pillar mountain—that was all. Mr. Jones had never visited Wastdale, and his work was unwritten. The entries in the climbers' book at the inn were only just begun.

W. P. Haskett Smith, J. W. Robinson, C. Slingsby, and G. Hastings were the pioneers of those days; they first really drew the attention of mountaineers to the fact that rock climbing of every degree of difficulty could be indulged in amongst the hills that surrounded the head of Wastdale.

It is true that for many years previously members of the Alpine Club had been in the habit of spending some time every year in the district, but they had gone there more for the ice and the snow and for the enjoyment of the mountain scenery than for indulgence in extraordinary performances in the ghylls and on the rock faces. May we not call theirs the Golden Age? whilst that sterner time which followed, full of fierce fighting, of victory and of defeat, was the Age of Iron.

It was my good fortune to be associated with those who were responsible for this second period, and many a long day have I spent on the mountains in their company. In those days at Easter time there was usually a great gathering of the mountaineering clans in the inn at Wastdale Head. They came from all points of the compass, and swooped down on Wastdale, bringing with them every sort of mountain appliance. Into the inn they would rush, soon to emerge again clothed in wonderful suits of clothes, carrying cameras, ropes, ice-axes, and luncheons; and they used to remind me of an instructive toy machine presented to a friend of mine in the days of his early youth—'morality made easy' he afterwards called it, when he had arrived at man's estate and was able to grasp the true inwardness of the ingenious apparatus. Its object was to inculcate at an early age the virtue of moderation, and it represented a public house. You slowly turned a handle, making a procession of respectably dressed citizens, with eager, smiling faces, enter the front door, over which was written in large letters:—

> 'They quietly enter the doorway within
> For an hour's indulgence in riot and sin.'

Another turn of the handle, which should now be done rapidly and with shaking hand, and at once the scene changed. From out the back door dishevelled and staggering figures emerged, with no resemblance whatever to the former ones. Above was another couplet :—

> 'Then rushing out wildly, their senses departed,
> On Ruin's dark pathway the victims are started!'

Alas! those delightful toys of one's youth, where have they all gone? The toys of the present day are feeble, and lack that educational value which those of thirty years ago never failed to possess. How can we compare them? It is *The Bad Boy's Book of Beasts* to Dr. Watts's *Poems.* The first of the two couplets mentioned above, in the case of the mountaineer, however, needs emendation; perhaps 'quiet lunchin'' at the end of the second line would be more appropriate. But I have wandered from my subject.

The inn at the head of Wastdale lies in the very centre of the hills, and from it two or three hours at the most will take the climber to his work.

On the south are the gullies of the Screes; the great gully opposite Wastdale Hall will occupy an ordinary party at least three hours. The first three or four hundred feet are by no means easy, and are thoroughly typical of ghyll climbing. On the south-east of Wastdale is Scawfell, with its splendid precipices where there are three first-rate ghyll climbs, Moss ghyll, Steep ghyll, and Deep ghyll. At the top of the last is Scawfell pinnacle, a delightful short climb if taken from the top of Scawfell; but if ascended from the foot of the precipice, *via* Steep ghyll, and then by the arête which lies between Steep ghyll and Deep ghyll, it will give several hours of really good rock work. Next to Scawfell are the Pikes and Great End. On both of these interesting scrambles can be found. To the eastward, almost above the inn, the slopes of Great Gable stretch up towards the Napes rocks, where can be found the Napes Needle and several rock ridges. Further away, on the north, lies the Pillar mountain, with its great buttress of rock jutting out into Ennerdale. Up the Pillar Rock there are at least half a dozen different routes, and none of them can be called perfectly easy. But these are by no means all the climbs that can be found near Wastdale Head. There are gullies on the Langdale Pikes and on Pavey Arc, and another on Dow Crag near Coniston.

My first climb was on the Napes Needle. Since then I have been up it many times, but it always remains as interesting as ever. I must confess that the first time I tried it, it was too difficult for me, and I was very glad of a helping hand from the first man up, for we were climbing without a rope and had no nails in our boots, our proper mountaineering equipment having been delayed at Drigg station; and as we afterwards learned, we had shocked Dan Tyson of the inn by going to the hills in what he considered were our Sunday clothes. But the Pillar Rock is the most famous crag near Wastdale. It lies on the far side of the Pillar mountain, and is not a great distance below the summit. It consists of a mass of rock standing far out from the side of the mountain, its precipices overhanging the head of Ennerdale. The end nearest the Pillar mountain is cut off from the hill-side by a great gash, whilst the other end plunges down almost perpendicularly for about eight hundred feet.

The great Ennerdale climb is up this Ennerdale face. At the bottom a broad grassy band, 'The Great Doupe,' runs across the foot of the precipice. It is from here that the climb must be begun, but every way up this face finally converges towards one spot, called the 'Split-Block.' Above is a vertical rock face, whilst below, four hundred feet straight down, is the grassy band. For nine years all attacks on the Ennerdale face of the Pillar Rock ended here. Only in 1891 was it conquered. Two of the party were lowered down into a savage-looking gully, from which they ascended to a spot some thirty feet higher than the Split-Block, and by lowering a rope were able to pull up the last man direct, who could not descend alone into the gully. This sounds as if the last man had a comparatively easy climb. But as the ascent is literally made through the air, unless an extra rope is sent down to help him with a noose at the end which can be used as a stirrup, he will arrive up above in a somewhat congested state. Moreover, he must insist that the two ropes be worked by reasonable people, otherwise he will be unfortunate enough to probably complete his ascent in an inverted position, and be apt to lose faith in the use of the Alpine rope.

It has already been pointed out that above the Split-Block is a vertical precipice. Across this face about twenty-five feet above the Split-Block there is another way up, which does away with the necessity of descending into the Savage gully. It was first climbed by G. Solly. But it is a most dangerous climb, for the leader must traverse across this perpendicular face hanging on by his hands alone, and—here is where the danger comes in—should he be unable to finish the climb, and the worst piece which needs the expenditure of most energy is at the very end, the leader is quite unable to return: there he hangs till he can hold on no longer, then he drops! I myself have seen this happen. The subsequent escape, not only of the leader but of the rest of the party, was the most marvellous piece of luck I have ever seen on the mountains, and even now makes me shudder when I think of it.

Collier has also varied this climb by getting up directly from the end of the ledge beyond the Split-Block; but, after all, the original manner employed by the first party in 1891 still remains the most satisfactory method for overcoming the difficulty at this spot on the Pillar climb. Above this, a gully leads to within two or three hundred feet of the top, which can be reached by an interesting rock climb of no great difficulty.

This ascent of the Pillar Rock is certainly a remarkably fine one. It is full of variety, and nearly the whole of it is on bare rock; moreover, owing to the great steepness during the greater part of the climb, it produces an exhilarating feeling of being perched in mid-air most of the time. I should think nowadays it cannot be difficult to find, but when we first tried it, a few scratches here and there on the rock were our only guides.

Of the ghyll climbs, the one on the Screes already mentioned is well worth trying. It was first climbed by Hastings, Robinson, and myself; and I could not have been in better company. Robinson is *the* great authority on the hills of the Lake district; there is not a rock on a mountain-side that he does not know. In sunshine or mist, in daylight or at midnight, he will guide one safely over passes or down precipitous mountain-sides. Every tree and every stone is a landmark to him. It was on a perfect winter's morning, many years ago now, that we started for the great gully in the Screes. Not a breath of air stirred; hoar frost covered the ground; the trees were a mass of silver, glittering in the morning sun. If from the road by Wastdale Hall the rock face opposite be examined, it does not seem to be much broken, but as one approaches the gullies deepen, and in reality are great gashes penetrating far into the hillside.

The bottom of the gully is reached by ascending a mass of loose stones which stretch almost down to the lake-side. In the gully there is no great difficulty at first, but after a short time it branches off into two, and it is the left-hand branch which has to be followed. The stream was frozen, forming a beautiful cascade of ice, and we were forced on to the buttress that divides the two gullies. Hastings was sent on to prospect, whilst I had to back him up as far as possible. With considerable trouble he managed to traverse back to the left into the main gully, using infinitesimal knobs of rock for foot and hand hold. We then followed, to find ourselves in a narrow cleft cut far into the side of the hill. Perpendicular walls rose on both sides for several hundred feet; above us stretched cascade after cascade of solid ice, always at a very steep angle and sometimes perpendicular. Up these we cut our way with our axes, sometimes being helped by making the steps close to the walls, and using any small inequalities on the rock face to steady us in our steps. At last we came to the final pitch. Far above us at the top, the stream coming over a hanging ledge on the right had frozen into masses of insecure icicles, some twenty or more feet long, and thus prevented us from getting up on that side. However, at the left-hand corner, at the top of the pitch, a rock was wedged, overhanging the gully, but leaving underneath a cave of considerable size. We managed to get as far up as the cave; there we placed Robinson, in a position of great importance and responsibility, for he had to hitch himself to a jammed boulder at the back, and hold both Hastings and me steady on the other end of the rope. I placed myself in the most secure position I could:

my right foot occupied a capacious hole cut in the bottom of the icicles, whilst my left was far away on the other side of the gully, on a small but obliging shelf in the rock face. In this interesting attitude, like the Colossus of Rhodes, I spanned the gulf, and was anchored to the boulder as well as to Robinson. Next, Hastings, with considerable agility, climbed on to my shoulders; from that exalted position he could reach the edge of the overhanging stone, underneath which Robinson was shivering, and, after great exertions, was able finally to pull himself up on to the top. Then Robinson and I followed on the rope. No doubt when the gully is dry, with neither ice nor water in it, the climb would be much modified. Above this pitch the climbing is easy as the gully opens out, and the route to the top may be varied according to taste; some ways are difficult and some are easy.

There is one more climb, the recollection of which always gives me pleasure; indeed it was one of the most delightful I ever had in this splendid land of rock scrambles. On the great precipice of Scawfell, Moss ghyll is the most easterly of the three gullies which look towards the Pikes.

When we attacked it, this ghyll had not been climbed, although several parties had been up a considerable distance. The highest point attained was just underneath a huge overhanging block of rock, weighing hundreds of tons, which formed the roof of a great cave. Robinson, Hastings, and I were anxious to see whether it was not possible in some way to circumvent this objectionable block. We had already carefully prospected the upper part of the ghyll from above, finding that there was no difficulty once this obstacle was passed. We therefore next attacked the ghyll from the bottom, hoping that we should be able to discover a way where others had failed.

Starting from below we chose the easiest route up the rock face on the right hand of the ghyll. Here the climbing chiefly consisted in getting from one ledge to another, up slabs of rock. We soon, however, got into the gully itself, where we found a perpendicular wall, up which we had to climb, before reaching a ledge, which the first party of exploration had called the 'Tennis Court' on account of its large size when compared with those lower down. If it were to grow vigorously, perhaps in its manhood it might become just large enough to run about on, but when we first made its acquaintance it must have been in its early childhood. From here we traversed back into the ghyll and got underneath the great overhanging block.

We found that below the great slab which formed

the roof another smaller one spanned the ghyll, forming the top of a great door to the cave behind. Under this we passed, and clambered up on to the top of it. Over our heads the great rock roof stretched some distance over the ghyll. Our only chance was to traverse straight out to the right, over the side of the ghyll, till one was no longer overshadowed by the roof above, and then, if possible, climb up the face of rock, and traverse back again above the obstacle into the ghyll once more.

This was easier to plan than to carry out; absolutely no handhold could be found, but only one little projecting ledge jutting out about a quarter of an inch and about a couple of inches long to stand on; moreover, a lip of rock overhung this little ledge, making it impossible to grip it satisfactorily with one's foot. Beyond this there were six or eight feet of the nearly perpendicular rock wall to traverse.

I was asked to try it. So, being highly pleased at being intrusted with such delicate operations, I with great deliberation stretched out my foot and tried to grip the little edge with the side nails of my boot. Just as I was going to put my whole weight on to this right foot, the nails, unable to hold on such a minute surface, gave way, and if Hastings had not instantly with a mighty pull jerked me back, I should have been swinging on the rope in mid-air. But we were determined not to be beaten. Hastings's ice-axe was next brought into requisition, and what followed I have no doubt will be severely criticised by more orthodox mountaineers than myself: as it was my suggestion I must take the blame. *I hacked a step in the rock!*[1] It was very hard work, but that upper lip to the step had to go, and Hastings's ice-axe, being an extraordinary one, performed its work admirably, and without damage to anything else than the rock. I then was able to get a much firmer foothold, and getting across this 'bad step,' clambered up the rock till I reached a spot where a capital hitch could be got over a jutting pin of rock, and the rest of the party followed. We then climbed out of the ghyll on the left up some slabs of rock.

A few days later, Moss ghyll was again climbed by a party led by J. Collier. They did not follow our track to the left after the overhanging rock had been passed, but climbed straight up, using a crack which looks almost impossible from below, thus adding an extra piece of splendid climbing to this expedition.

[1] During climbing in ice and snow one is allowed, in fact, one is expected, to cut steps. But it is held to be entirely contrary to the laws which govern the great sport of mountaineering to make similar holes in rock. This is remarkable, though nevertheless true.

That Collier did not follow our route was, I believe, entirely due to Robinson, who, being so excessively delighted with having at last conquered Moss ghyll, wrote a long account of it in the climbing book at the inn, and being in this particular instance far more capable of successfully climbing Moss ghyll than describing how it was done, produced a tale where the points of the compass got, so to speak, 'snarked.'

But to return to our climb: just as it was getting dark we emerged on to the top of Scawfell. The sun-god had plunged once more into the baths of ocean, leaving behind him the golden splendour of a perfect evening. In the far distance lay the sea, with banks of sullen mist brooding over it; nearer, like a purple curtain, stretched the low hills by the coast; whilst far away in the south, towering into the sunset glow, out of a level surface of sea mists rose the peaks of Snowdon and the two Carnedds in Wales.

Towards the east, range after range of mountain crests encompassed the horizon as far as the eye could see, from the Yorkshire moors, with their strong, massive outline crowned by Ingleboro and Whernside, to Skiddaw and the Scotch hills beyond the sands of the Solway.

Delicate pearl-grey shadows creep in amongst

the wealth of interlacing mountain forms in the clear air, deepening towards the far east into the darkness of approaching night. No sound breaks the stillness, all around are piled the tumbled fragments of the hills, hoary with the memories of forgotten years. The present fades away, and is lost in the vast ocean of time; a lifetime seems a mere shadow in the presence of these changeless hills. Slowly this inscrutable pageant passes, but blacker grow the evening shadows; naught remains but the mists of the coming night, and darkness soon will fall upon this lonely mountain-land.

'A land of old, upheaven from the abyss
By fire, to sink into the abyss again;
Where fragments of forgotten peoples dwelt,
And the long mountains ended in a coast
Of ever-shifting sand, and far away
The phantom circle of a moaning sea.'

A REVERIE

> . . . Restless thoughts, that, like a deadly swarm
> Of hornets arm'd, no sooner found alone,
> But rush upon me thronging, and present
> Times past.'
>
> MILTON.

On winter evenings, when out of doors the fogs and dirt of London reign supreme, it is the wisest course to sit at home in one's arm-chair, warmed by the blaze of a comfortable fire, and with some favourite book for a companion, to watch the smoke curl upwards from one's pipe. But after a time the book falls on to one's knees, and all sorts and conditions of pictures float lazily through the tobacco mists. I have been told that effects are due to causes. Perhaps these undisciplined wanderings of my brain may be only the inevitable result of a good dinner; perhaps the quiet content that I feel may be caused only by a spirit of contradiction—a knowledge that the arm-chair and the desultory visions of my brain should be ruthlessly put aside, to give place to exact, well-regulated thoughts concentrated on necessary labour. Be it what it may, I will not work to-night. A nebulous peace of mind has claimed and absorbed me which it would be impious to dispel. I shall let my memory lift the curtain behind which lies the past.

The thousand and one small duties of the present, mostly absurd trivialities, the insignificance of which is only equalled by their persistence, can be neglected for once, and shall be as dust in the balance, without weight to disturb the equipoise of my mind. Letters from people I do not know, requesting information on subjects that do not concern me—letters which, as far as I can see, merely stamp the writers as belonging to that class of human animal incapable of thinking for itself—these shall remain unanswered. Why should such shallow creatures be allowed to worry the more robust portion of the universe by their energetic yet irritating display of letter-writing? why have I to spend much ink and thought in answering them? Truly this is a weary world! Man is born to trouble as the sparks fly upwards. Worries and bothers are for ever at one's elbow.

But here I am thus early inveighing against the petty annoyances of the present instead of enjoying those reminiscences of former years that, viewed through the mists of time, have their pleasures enhanced and their pains discounted; when I can allow my memory a free field from which it may pick the fairest flowers that have blossomed in those bygone years.

Ah! a quotation comes wandering by: when it is at home it may be found in an 'Ode to the Terrestrial Globe,' by an unhappy wretch:—

> 'It's true my prospects all look blue—
> But don't let that unsettle you!
> Never you mind.
> Roll on!' (*It rolls on.*)

And as it rolls on down the distances of my mind, it leaves me, being in a very contrary frame of mind, somewhat comforted. Moreover, it opens up new channels for thought, and those exquisite lines on golf that occur somewhere in *Paradise Lost* are of course at once suggested, but I am too lazy to find the context:—

> 'So eagerly with horrid voice the Fiend
> Cries "Fore!" as he o'er the far bunker drives
> The errant ball; it with the setting sun
> Dropp'd from the zenith like a falling star,
> Alas! untruly urged, it lies in Hell.'

Then I muse over all the golf-courses that I have played on or seen, from St. Andrews to an improvised one above Astor amongst the stately pines on the Himalayan mountains, when the snow peaks and the glaciers, glistening in the marvellous sunshine, play hide-and-seek with the white fleecy clouds that drift over their summits.

Those wonderful mountains! what magnificent outlines, what grandeur, what mystery, what! . . . Stop! can I be growing sentimental? It must have been the dinner that has produced this particular physiological sensation.

However, the sensation is passing, and my thoughts have flown back naturally to the subject of dinners. Yes, many dinners—what a subject! —glorious, unapproachable, exhaustless dinners! I could write pages, volumes, in praise of dinners; but not for the vulgar, not for the uninitiated—that surely were sacrilege. Dinners that with subtle and insinuating address came and went, leaving behind them fascinating and precious memories, even though 'good digestion did not wait on appetite.' Dinners, too, eaten under the stars. Yes, now I think of it, that *was* a dinner! when four of us ate a whole sheep, after two weary days and nights spent starving on the icy slopes of Nanga Parbat.

Mountaineering, truly thou art a marvellous and goodly provoker of hunger! Those mortals who may be in search of sensations—big, boisterous, blustering sensations not to be denied—should sacrifice often on thy altars, O Goddess of the Hills!

In the mountains, however, these sensations, these inspired ecstasies of mind and body, may be pushed sometimes rather far; then the recoil comes, and with it contrast, which however is often agreeable. But these memories of unpleasant Alpine half-hours grow faint as one sits in a satisfying arm-chair—they are easily discounted in a process of mental dissipation, by which one cheats oneself; and finally, it is easy to believe that there is no sport like mountaineering. Of course this conclusion is fallacious—conclusions sometimes are. Again my thoughts are interrupted. Outside in the cold, the rain, and the darkness some poor wretch is making night hideous by attempting to sing—

'There is a 'appy land, for for awye.'

Most true! most philosophical! The Islands of the Blest usually are some distance away. We have been told by the poet that neither are they to be attained by omnibuses, nor to be approached by

'A ram-you-damn-you liner with a brace of bucking screws.'

Therefore why disturb the darkness, O most miserable one, by dismal reiteration of a well-known fact? But still the song moans out its Cockney dialect, false notes, and falser sentiment; and the singer, drenched to the skin, possibly starving, with probably only one desire, and that for drink, goes his way. I hear the melancholy music die into the distance. Of a truth his sensations cannot be pleasant; but with these few coppers changed into the equivalent of alcohol perhaps he also may

'Life's leaden metal into gold transmute,'

and cheat himself into the belief that life is worth living. That last sentence, now I come to read it over again, seems perhaps a trifle cynical; *seems*, certainly, but are we not told that things often 'are not what they seem'? I have heard the late poet laureate accused (and by a Scotchwoman, too!) of writing slang.

'Did I look on great Orion sloping slowly towards the west.'

My thoughts, too, are 'sloping' in a westerly direction. I am on a personally-conducted tour—my brain is in command, and I am the spectator.

If only I can forget that those letters have to be answered, and if no other miserable wretch comes to sing touching refrains outside in the rain, my brain and I shall thoroughly enjoy each other's company; whilst the firelight sheds its dim radiance over glimpses of the metamorphised past and the indeterminable future, till all is so blended together that I cannot tell whether these things have been or are to be.

I see long stretches of Rannoch moor as Stevenson saw it, 'where the mists rise and die away, and showed us that country lying as waste as the sea; only the moorfowl and the peewees crying upon it, and far over to the east a herd of deer moving like dots. Much of it is red with heather; much of the rest broken up with bogs and hags and peaty pools; some had been burnt black in a heath fire; and in another place there are quite a forest of dead firs, standing like skeletons.'

Northward over the moor ponderous Ben Alder lifts his bleak and barren top in massive strength above lonely Loch Ericht, whilst beyond the loch, Schehallion's slender summit, deep blue in the evening sky, tells of that fierce day when the body of the dead Graham lay on the hillside and the sun went down on a lost cause.

Southward are the peaks of the Black Mount and the peaceful hills that feed the upper waters of Glen Lyon; then Buchaille Etive and all those wild, rocky mountains further west, dominating wild Glencoe, stir the memory with the story of how Campbell of Glen Lyon betrayed and murdered the whole of the M'Ians with treachery as black as the cliffs of the Aonach Dubh and as cruel as the winter winds that sweep mercilessly across the corries and pinnacles of Bidean nam Bian, the peak of the storms. Or in imagination I follow Alan Breck with Davie Balfour as they flee by the sea-loch that separates Appin from Mamore up and across to the great moor, toiling and resting, but ever onward, till amongst the labyrinth of glens in the heart of the forest of Ben Alder they found Cluny Macpherson. Yes, Rannoch moor is wild and desolate; and could the grey blocks of stone or the bare slabs of granite that lie amongst the brown heather speak, surely there would be many more tales of bygone adventures to listen to and wonder over.

From Rannoch my mind wanders across the stretches of blue water, past stormy Ardnamurchan to the island of Mull. I am on the summit of Ben More; below lies a ridge smothered in snow and ice. I am trying all I can with words of sweet persuasion to entice my companion, Colin Phillip, down what is obviously the shortest route to the next peak, A Chioch. But he says it is impossible, he will not trust himself on that slope of snow and ice. Now my thoughts fly to the shores of Loch Earn. I am listening to one, a geologist, who expounds to me the marvels of the prehistoric glacier; he also, with words of sweet persuasion, is trying to make me believe that Loch Morar was excavated by a glacier. Those wonderful geological truths, how simple, how all-sufficient they are to explain to the uninitiated the why and wherefore of the ancient mountains; but put not your trust in them; they suffer by the process of evolution, and are changed. Without doubt, in those days Phillip believed that I was totally ignorant of mountaineering; whilst now, perhaps, that geologist thinks that I am equally ignorant of the truth. Whether it is the truth about Loch Morar that I mean, or about that geologist's statement, or about my own, I really don't know.

In imagination I am hurried on; I see myself, footsore and weary, wandering through Ardgour and Moidart, or across from Invercannich through Affric's wild glens down to Shiel House, by the western sea; now I am glissading down Beinn Alligin, or hacking my way through a cornice, apparently hundreds of feet high, on Aonach Mor, my companion Travers meanwhile slowly freezing on the brink of an *absolutely* perpendicular ice slope, the daylight waning, and our retreat cut off. Then comes a glimpse of the platform at Kingshouse station. I am addressing winged words to Colin Phillip, and he is engaged in a contentious refutation of my argument. The subject is not at all interesting—only the comparative usefulness of painting and photography as a means for reproducing mountain form; but the result is most disgraceful, for presently we are seen sitting at different ends of the platform waiting for the train, and thinking—well, it doesn't matter what we thought. Was it yesterday, or when, that all these things happened? Still it cannot be so very long ago that Phillip climbed Sgurr Alasdair, the finest peak of the Coolin in Skye. Would that on that occasion, just below the summit, I had possessed a camera, for then could I have shown Phillip that photography at least was capable of very faithfully reproducing his manly and superior form, as he was seen approaching the cairn, even though it might be useless in giving us the true proportions of inferior mountains. Neither do I think that I should be overstepping the bounds of prudence should I assert that Colin Phillip has a marked dislike for stone walls. I have hopes, however, that some day a happy combination of the despised camera—the stone wall and Phillip—may yield interesting results. Little did Phillip think, that evening at Kingshouse, that a time would come when the maligned camera would turn—turn its eye on Phillip and on that stone wall—and wink with malicious pleasure.

But in spite of winged words, weary feet, and endless eggs and bacon, these were fine times—from Sutherland to the Galloway Highlands, from Mull to the mountains on Deeside, Colin Phillip and I have wandered in fair weather and in foul.

We have waxed enthusiastic over the Cairngorm mountains. We have watched the last light of day fade far away over the Atlantic behind the islands of the west; and although we may have disagreed in many things, yet we have always acknowledged that for wild beauty, for colour, for atmospheric effects and lonely grandeur, we know of no country that is equal to the Highlands of Scotland.

But a younger century has arrived, and

> 'The old order changeth, yielding place to new.'

Somewhere have I seen some remarks about the Coolin, where no mention is made of the mountains as being capable of stirring the imagination or gratifying the mind; no, the subject was 'the ridiculously easy nature of the climbing in Skye,' 'the gabbro of the Coolin being too good,' and so on, the New Mountaineer merely looking upon these peaks and ribs of splintered rock as a useful spot where gymnastic feats might be performed, and even compares the Coolin unfavourably with the decomposing granite slabs at the head of Glen

S

Sannox. Truly the glory of the mountains is departing. The progressive, democratical[1] finger of the 'New Mountaineer' is laid with equal irreverence and mockery on Sgurr nan Gillean and Cir Mhor, and this spirit of irresponsible criticism 'fulfils itself in many ways.' It is not the first time that the Coolin have been 'slandered.' Have they not been called 'inferior mountains'? (*Modern Painters*). Now the climbers 'run' over the Pinnacle Ridge of Sgurr nan Gillean, and no doubt the next generation (if they have wise fathers) will be induced to take their maternal grandmothers up the inaccessible summit of Sgurr Dearg. One by one the recollections of all our most cherished climbs will be punctured, flat and unprofitable as a collapsed bicycle tire; they will rotate over the rough roads of bygone memories, whilst that progressive democratical finger will guide the new nickel-plated, pneumatic-cushioned, electrically-driven modern mountaineer on his fascinating career. But to return. I am still sitting in my comfortable armchair, and looking at my own fingers to see whether they possess a progressive democratical appearance.

Before me passes the vision of a mountain, a beautiful, many-headed mountain, hidden away

[1] 'They are still within the line of vulgarity, and are *democratical* enemies of truth.'—Browne's *Vulg. Errours.*

from democratical enemies of mountaineering, and without the line of vulgarity. Carefully enclosed on its western face lies a corrie named Coire Mhic Fhearchair. I see a party wandering up its glacier-worn entrance. At its head the mist lies low down, but not low enough to hide the precipices that encircle the lochan in its centre. On the right, snow-filled gullies sweep with graceful curves from a dome-shaped peak.

But it is the rock escarpment at the back of the corrie that fascinates their gaze. As the mists begin to clear one by one, they suggest climbs on its face, for there are 1250 feet of bare rock in front of them, broken up into three distinct buttresses with two splendid gullies dividing them. At last they choose the right-hand gully, and, having roped themselves, proceed to cut steps up the steep snow that has drifted into it and obliterated any perpendicular pitches there may be. I am sorry that there are no perpendicular pitches—it is most unfortunate; for I should like to see that party performing all these daring feats so well known to, and beloved by, the professional rock climber. 'How things began to look rather blue.' 'How for a minute or two one of the party remained spread-eagled on the face of a cliff almost despairing of getting up, the desired crack being a good two feet out of reach, till, with a supreme effort, he was propelled from below by a sudden and powerful jerk, his outstretched fingers seize the desired crack.' Nor can I describe how 'the heavy man of the party, his finger tips playing upon the face of the cliff with the delicacy of touch of a professional pianist, his every movement suggestive of the bounding lightness of the airy thistle-down,' followed. No, I am sorry I have no such wildly exciting adventures to relate, nor such poetical fancies wherewith to eke out a plain story. I see that party merely climbing up that gully, in a most uninteresting yet simple manner, by cutting steps. They come to where it ends against a perpendicular and overhanging cliff at least a couple of hundred feet high. Only 200 feet, but higher they cannot go, for none of the party are sufficiently muscular to propel the leader with a jerk upwards that paltry 200 feet. Therefore they climb out to their left, along a narrow and somewhat broken ledge, on to the middle buttress, where a place is found large enough for them all to sit down. They gaze upwards at the last 300 feet that separate them from the summit, but it is steep, very steep, 'A.P.'[1] Also, it is late in the afternoon; so they comfort themselves by building

[1] *Absolutely* perpendicular.

a cairn, and eating all these delicious things that are so good on a mountain-side—meat sandwiches which have remained from lunch, and taste so full of mustard and so delightfully dry; old, old prunes encrusted with all kinds of additional nutriment from the bottom of some one's pocket; a much-worn stick of chocolate, or perhaps an acidulated drop—on such fare does the hardy mountaineer feed. I see them once more in the gully, but they descend more rapidly than they climbed up it, for the more daring of the party glissade down the lower part, and so home.

On the morrow, however, I see three of the party again setting forth for that precipice. This time, instead of approaching it from the north-west by the Allt Toll a'Ghiubhais, they hire a 'machine, and drive as far as the foot of Sgurr Bàn on the southern side; then mounting to the peak just to the west of Sgurr Bàn by a well-made deer path, they soon arrive at the summit of the middle buttress, overlooking Coire Mhic Fhearchair. They climb out to the very end of the nose and look down, straight below, and only 300 feet away is the little cairn built on the preceding afternoon, but, as I have remarked before, that 300 feet is very steep. A photograph taken from the most southerly of the three buttresses, so as to get the middle buttress in profile, shows the angle of the last 200 feet to be about 85 degrees, not quite but very nearly 'A.P.' However, they think that they may as well see how far they can descend. The rocks on the left-hand (southern) side of the buttress are obligingly broken up, so that by a series of small climbs the party are enabled to get from one small platform to the next, always edging towards the outside of the buttress. At last they all congregate together. A perpendicular slab, which has partly come away from the front of the crags, bars their way to the right, and, below, a quite perpendicular drop of about 200 feet on to the ledge quietly but firmly impresses on them the fact that that way is not for them. But always in mountaineering, just as things become quite hopeless and 'blue,' then it is the duty of the person who describes the adventure to appeal to the feelings of the public (who, presumably, are unacquainted with that particular climb). It is his duty to picture these unfortunate individuals, fearful that their retreat is cut off, yet unable to proceed; how, having dangled on the ends of ropes, swinging backwards and forwards in the breeze, they return to the ledge baffled; or having climbed on each other's shoulders, they find 'the desired crack two good feet out of reach,' and there is not always one in the party powerful enough to 'propel' the leader 'from below by a sudden and powerful jerk, so that he can with outstretched fingers clutch that desired crack.' But still, with a little imagination, we can see these things. A good imagination is necessary, I may say very necessary, to the enthusiastic climber; much pleasure is otherwise lost.

The party I see, evidently has none of this precious imagination. They are obviously wasting their opportunities most shamefully on that rock face. I see one of them climb out on to the face just under the great loose slab, and disappear round the corner; then the rest follow, and find themselves on the topmost of a series of ledges, and about 200 feet above the small cairn below. I will not describe that traverse, but will merely mention that the party seem quite pleased with it. Then they begin the descent. First they get down a narrow slit between a slab and the buttress, and with a drop of about 10 feet get into the next ledge. Next they have to climb down another slab, bulging over into space, or a perpendicular gully gives them an interesting piece of climbing. About 120 feet from the bottom they build a small cairn, and then, without much further difficulty, they finally find themselves where they had ended their climb on the afternoon of the day before. They do not, however, descend to the bottom of the gully, but about half-way down, traversing out to the left, they make for the ridge connecting Sail Mhòr with the rest of the mountain. It is now evening, and I ought, if orthodox, here 'to burst out in sentences which swell to paragraphs, and in paragraphs which spread over pages; to plunge into ecstasies about infinite abysses and overpowering splendours, to compare mountains to archangels, lying down in eternal winding-sheets of snow, and to convert them into allegories about man's highest destinies and aspirations. This is good when it is well done. Yet most humble writers will feel that if they try to imitate Mr. Ruskin's eloquence, they will pay the penalty of becoming ridiculous. It is not every one who can with impunity compare Alps to archangels.'[1] Yet there is always something about sunsets which is horribly fascinating—from a literary point of view; it is so easy to become suddenly enthusiastic and describe how 'The sun-god once more plunges into the baths of ocean.' The sea too is always useful at such moments. 'Banks of sullen mist, brooding like a purple curtain,' etc., sounds well; and one must not forget 'the shadows of approaching night,'—they form a fitting background for the gloomy and introspective spirit which

[1] *The Playground of Europe.*—Leslie Stephen.

ought to seize upon one at this particular psychological moment. 'The tumbled fragments of the hills, hoary with memories of forgotten years,' come next, with a vague suggestion of solitude, which should be further emphasised by allusions to 'the present fading away, and being lost in the vast ocean of time, a lifetime being merely a shadow in the presence of these changeless hills.' Then, to end up, mass the whole together, and call it an 'inscrutable pageant'; pile on the shadows, which must grow blacker and blacker, till 'naught remains but the mists of the coming night and darkness'; and if you have an appropriate quotation, put it in!

THE OROMANIACAL QUEST

To all ingeniously elaborate students in the most divine mysteries of the oromaniacal quest: an account in which is set forth the eminent secrets of the adepts; whereunto is added a perfect and full discoverie of the way to attaine to the Philosopher's heavenly chaos.

'Whose noble practise doth them teach
To vaile their secrets wyth mystie speach.'
The Hunting of the Greene Lyon.

After that the three most respectable Travellers and Searchers after vast protuberances of the earth, in the land of the Caledones, had with haste, joyousness, and precision arrived at those parts, where with observation, snow-covered mountains together with rocks and ice in abundance, and also many other things may be perceived which commend themselves to true worshippers of that most mystagorical and delectable pursuit—the oromaniacal Quest into the secret and hidden Mysteries of sublime Mountains—they at once determined to so haste, walk, run, climb, and otherwise betake themselves to the uppermost parts of the hills, that by continual patience a new entrance towards the topmost pinnacle should be discovered, which should in all respects yield that quintessential pleasure they believed could be extracted from such pursuit of the enigmatical Process.

There be, however, many who deny that the Quintessence of the true enjoyment can so be attained. These indeed do maintain that it resides in that subtill art, the striking of a ball violently with a stick, but this also is a mystery; therefore I will not launch my little skiff further into the wide ocean of the dispute, neither will I argue with such fellows, for do they not offend philosophically, and therefore should be admonished to the end that they meddle not with the Quest of the true Brethren?

Thou askest, Why? I say thou hast not tasted of these things! Hast thou not tarried with those that are below, or, ascending, hast thou not proceeded upwards by help of mules, jackasses, and other auxiliaries, or even in these swift, luxurious and delectable vehicles drawn by the demon of water ten times heated in the furnace? I bid thee search that treasure-house of clouds, fountains, fogs, and steep places on thine own ten toes, and peradventure thou shalt find that which is above resembleth not that which is beneath, neither are the high places of the earth like unto the groves and hedgerows, or the places where people do most congregate, in towns, villages, courts, gardens, to the end that they may hold discourse, spagyrising, philosophising, lanternising, whereby is the engendering of fools a most mystical matter furthered—also the concocting of many poculations; truly these fellows are vulgar tosspots, they attaine not the first Matter, nor the whole operation of the Work; neither do they approach to the enchanted Treasure-House sought for by that worthy Quintessencer and most respectable Traveller, Master Beroalde of fragrant and delectable memory.[1] Also are these fellows most injurious to well-deserving Philosophers, for they comprehend not the writings, and through 'misunderstanding of the possibilities of Nature do commit foul mistakes in their operations, and therefore reap a ridiculous harvest.' Our Record is writ neither for simple, vulgar, and pitiful sophisters, nor for such owls, bats, and night-birds, who, blinded by the full light of the Quest lye hidden in gloomy nooks, crannies, and holes below.

But return we to our purpose. When our three travellers had arrived at that place in the northland, hight Castrum Guillelmi, they tarried there awhile seeking diligently if perchance even in that place the great Mysterie, the quintessential Pleasure of devout Philosophers, could by searching be

[1] The Spagyric Quest of Beroaldus Cosmopolita.

attained. 'Good,' said they; 'Now are we near the Fulfilment, the Entrance into Secret Places, the Consummation, the Marriage of the Impossible with the Real, the Knowledge of this Mastery.' So it came to pass that on the day following, early and with great joyousness, did they start forth by the straight road.

Nor did they issue forth unprepared, for they bore with them the proper, peculiar, fit, exact, and lawful insignia of the brotherhood, a mystic thread, coiled even as the sable serpent, likewise staves curiously shapen did they take in their hands, for 'peradventure,' said they, 'the way may be steep and full of toil, the dangers many; behold go we not forth in a savage land, where liveth the white dragon and eke basilisks, spoken of by the ingenious J. J. Scheuchzerus, doctor of medicine, what time he did wander in the far country of the Helvetii? Good, now come we to it! for saith not Aristotle in his *Physicks*, "*Ab actionibus procedit speculatio*," "Now are all things propitious, let us seek the Delphinian oracle"; Phœbus like unto the fiery Dragon shines bravely, conquering the hydropical vapours and transforming them into subtill aerial sublimations; soon shall we come to the high places where abideth the great water the Lochan Meal an't Suidhe. It shall we leave on the dexter hand, for the path lieth not there but onwards, straight without twist or turn along the valley at the feet of the red Mountains, whose hue is multiplied, transmuted, and purified even unto seven times seven, a wonder to the sight, and tincted by the ruddy colour of Sol the golden, what time he goeth down at eventide, slavering the deep waters of the western sea so that they be all of a gore bloud.'

But let not these things turn us from the true Quest, the hidden Mysteries, which in the opinion of the vulgar rude are by many deemed nought but delusions. For over against and opposite across the valley, abideth the Immensity of greatness, the majestic Silence, the prodigious Dampness, the Depth, in shape like a great Dome, whereof the base is in the Flouds and the Waters, whence issueth forth delectable springs welling up for ever, continually ascending yet ever flowing downwards; here perchance shall we find the Mysterie of the heavenly Chaos, and the great Abyss, the way to attaine to Happiness, even the quintessential mystagorical Delight and oromaniacal Quest, so highly extolled yet so deeply concealed by the true Philosophers.

Thus did they fare onward toward the midst of the valley placed between the red Hill and the great Mountain. Then behold before them rose hugeous rocks and bulky stones standing on end facing to the north where the ice and snow tarry from one winter even unto the following; for in those places the sun shines not, neither are found the comfortable, soft, juicy, and fœculent breezes of the South ; there the brood of the black Crow and the white smoak or vapour, and comprehensive congelations of the Mistus Scotorum are produced. So were the Brethren sore amazed, but as yet could not see even the first matter of the Work.

'See,' said one, 'the way leadeth upward where the Spirit arising like unto a volatisation, a separation or sublimation or wind, has much bewhited the mighty petrolific ridge full of points towers and pinnacles. There the pursuit may be pursued, there the volatisation which is an ascension may be compleatly demonstrated, and the operation of the great Work may be begun. First must we fashion in the snow and ice great stairs of steps, by aid of which, through prolongation, extension, reduplication, and multiplication shall we be brought on to the Ridge even at the beginning.' So did they enter upon the Work in this lowest period of obscurity, multiplying the steps in a certain mystic manner which had been revealed to them; and it came to pass that they attained at last on to the Ridge, whereon might be perceived far above, towers, pinnacles, points, and other pleasant places, suitable and useful for the furtherance of the Quest.

First did they traverse a narrow edge of snow fashioned by the wind. Then said one, 'Follow me, but look not either to the right or to the left, for there lyeth the Abyss.' So they followed him, with the mystic thread fastened to their girdles. They saw how that, far above, the heavens were separated from the white snow, which was curled and twisted, also falling, overhanging, and extended, so that they could perceive no way whereby they might pass through.

But above and beyond lay the summit of the great Mountain, where clouds are concocted in the natural furnace; there also may be seen in the proper season, 'The whole operation of the Sons of Wisdom, the great Procession and the Generation of Storms, the Marriage of the Stars and the Seven Circulations of the Elements.' So did they fare onwards; and by inspection were they aware how others had travelled on the same way, for on the stones and rocks were certain petrographical scratchings and curious markings deeply graven and very evident. But presently came they to a great Rock, a majestic Tower. Here were they perforce compelled to depart to the right hand, placing themselves in steep and perilous positions on slopes of ice, which downwards seemed to end in empty air, even in the great void.

Then were the Three exceeding joyful, for is it not written in the secret books of the Brethren, Many operations must they perform amidst the great mountains and the snowy ice, especially and creditably, ere they be so transmuted, mystagorified and metagrabolised, that they may be numbered with the True, the Pious, the Elect, even amongst those who are considered worthy of the most mystical and allegorical symbol, A.C., by many variously interpreted. For some hold that it signifies, 'Adepti Cragorum,' whilst others 'Angelorum Confederatio,' for these latter maintain that the Quest can only be rightly pursued, or satisfactorily continued, by the aid of wings; but in this matter they are deceived, and argue foolishly after the wisdom of the flesh. Still all things have an end at last—good Wine, Pinnacles, Spires, cabalistic Emblems, and oromaniacal Wanderings, even the green sauce of the Philosophers and the pythagoric Mustard of the Great Master himself, spoken of by Alcofribas Nasier in his merrie work. So did the Three find the perilous passage across the headlong steep of that ruinous place finish.

Then did they pass onward to the Labyrinth, the rocky chaos, and greatly did they marvel at the exceeding steepness thereof; so that only by great perseverance, turning now to the left and now to the right, were they able to break themselves free from the bonds and entanglements, and climb sagaciously upwards to the summit of the great Tower. Whereon did they find a heaped up accumulation of stones curiously erected, a cabalistic Pyramid, set there doubtless by a former seeker in the Work, to the end that true searchers might not despair, but continue the matter of the Work with fresh hope and industry. But when they had gazed for a short space, they perceived how that the Consummation, the great Fulfilment, was nigh at hand. Behind and far below, imprinted in the snow, were the steps by which they had mounted upwards, winding now this way, now that, looking like scarce seen veins in whitest marble. But before them lay the narrow Way, the Ridge, the Cleft, and the White Slope, leading even unto the utmost Height, the sovereign Summit of the mightie Mountain. Thither therefore did their footsteps trend.

First did they pass along the narrow Way,

treading with exceeding care and exactness, for there was but foothold for one alone; the path being no broader than a man's hand. Next did they descend into the Cleft, which thing is also emblematical and symbolical of the precious secret of all Philosophies, for without this key can no one unlock the Hermetic Garden, the Arcanum of the Alchemists, spoken of by Paracelsus in his *Archidoxis*.

Now before them stretched the white Slope, which lay beneath the topmost summit, and steeper became the path, going upwards with a great steepness; now whilst the three Travellers did toil and seek, endeavouring to meet the perils of the way, yet almost despairing, lo! from out the clouds a thread descended and a voice was heard afar off: 'Fear not, now have ye attained to the Consummation, enter into the mystagorical, quintessential, and delectable Pleasure-House of devout Oromaniacs!'

Thus therefore do the true Philosophers distinguish that which is superior from that which is inferior, for it is a thing deeply concealed by the envious, let therefore the same be thy subject to work upon, thy first Basis, for the white must first come out of the red, and black following with multiplicative virtue rise above according to the nature of all things. Hear then the meaning of the four Degrees. Thy first Degree maketh to sweat but gently. In the second much travail followeth, whereby thy sweat increaseth, whilst *tertius excedit et cum tolerantia laedit*, for our way ascendeth speedilie where the black rocks fall and rise continually. Congelation and Circulation cometh next, when in the fourth Degree the blackness wears away, which, believe me, is a gallant sight. 'Then shalt thou see thy Matter appear, shining, sparkling, and white even like to a most glorious heaven-born Mercury the subject of wonders. Then if thou art fortunate shall the fumes cease and our congelation will glitter incomparably and wonderfully, and thickening more and more it will sprout like the tender frost in a most amiable lustre. Now thou needest no further instruction, only this let me tell you, understand this well, and you will not be amazed any longer with the distinction of our Operations. For all is but a successive action and passion of him who seeks for the Work. Which carrying him up and down like a wheel, returns thither whence it proceeded, and then beginneth again and turns so long till it finds its rest So he thus attains a *plusquam* perfection through the marvellous co-operation of Art and Nature.'[1]

[1] *The First Gate.* By the Chanon of Bridlington.

'Who knoweth not this in knowledge is blind,
He may forth wander as mist in the wind,
Wotting never with profit where to light,
Because he understands not our words aright.'

Therefore, with what joy, think you, did the Three progress onward after the long and troublous ascent? After *scrambling*,

slipping,	*gathering,*
pulling,	*talking,*
pushing,	*stepping,*
lifting,	*grumbling,*
gasping,	*anathematising,*
looking,	*scraping,*
hoping,	*hacking,*
despairing,	*bumping,*
climbing,	*jogging,*
holding on,	*overturning,*
falling off,	*hunting,*
trying,	*straddling,*
puffing,	*and at last*
loosing,	*attaining,*

for know ye that by these methods alone are the most divine Mysteries of the Quest reached.

So at last they came even unto the very topmost Point, and were aware how that Priests from the heavenly Temple, which is placed on the top of that Mountain, had come forth to guide them, without further difficulty, across a level plain of white snow to the gates of the Temple itself. But the perils of the way were not ended. At the threshold were there many steps leading down and underground to the Temple's innermost recesses, through a domed vault or doorway built of the plastered snow. Now were these steps both slippery and very treacherous, having been fashioned in a truly sopho-spagyric manner, likewise did they seem reduplicated and multiplied even by the Pythagorical Tetrad. Moreover, above the portal were there magical characters engraven, even after the same fashion as those seen by the wise Pantagruel what time he sought the Oracle of the Bottle in the land of Lanterns.

But beyond the portal a very thick mistie and cimmerian darkness, an eclipsation, apprehended them, and the Three did stumble now this way and now that, so did they greatly fear even at this very end of their Quest, that beasts and creeping things of monstrous shape awaited them, dangers far worse than those on the steep places of the Mountain.

'Art thou here?' said one. 'Prithee guide my steps!' quoth another. 'Alas, we are undone!' cried a third. 'Zoons, why are ye afraid?' answered a voice; 'when ye have passed the three-square Corner and the Darkness ye are safe in the Sanctum Sanctorum even of the Elect, in the Philosopher's heavenly Chaos, where may ye understand all Mysteries. But first answer ye me, whence come ye?' 'From without and below.' 'And how?' 'By the seven-fold stairs nigh unto the great Abyss where liveth the brood of the black Crow, and the engendering of the Mistus Scotorum proceedeth perpetually.' 'Good, but how did ye proceed?' 'Thence came we by the rocky Labyrinth, and by the perilous Passage to the great Tower, and the mystic Pyramid, which is set on the further side of the narrow Way and the Cleft, emblematic of hidden things; thence by the white Slope to the topmost Summit. So have we sought the divine mysteries of this great Quest with much toil, so may we attaine to the Philosopher's heavenly Chaos.'

Then said the voice, 'Enter into the abode of Knowledge, through the open Entrance to the shut Palace of the King,[1] into the outer chamber of the most sophistical Retreat of the Sons of Wisdom, where are perpetually and endlessly produced many reasonable meteorological prognostications; also divinations, concentrations, observations, and conglomerations are recorded in divers registers,

[1] Introitus apertus ad occlusum Regis palatium.

all of them most deducible, for are they not stored with great care in sundry leathern bags for the delectation of wise men? Thou hast been led as it were by the hand through many a desert and waste spot, now lift up your eyes and behold where you are; welcome into the garden of the Philosophers, which is walled about with a very high wall.' So were they shown by the dwellers in the Temple many and marvellous wonders. In the centre stood a furnace for all transmutations and agitations by heat; whilst on shelves did they see great store of divers bottles, pans, boxes, and bags, wherein could be found succulent sauces and philosophical essences, to the end that the delectable concoctions of the pious might be completed.

Likewise great numbers of books. In some could be found treatises of the true science, also devices, hieroglyphic interpretations and perspicuous renderings of great wisdom, in others histories of joyous diversions. Also were there 'curious and ingenious engines for all sorts of motions, where were represented and imitated all articulate sounds and letters, and conveyed in trunks and strange lines and distances. Also helps for the sight representing things afar off in the heavens and remote places, as near, and making feigned distances.'[1] Likewise mathematical instruments, exquisitely made, for the discovering of small and minute bodies in the air. 'Also divices for natural divination of tempests, great inundations, temperatures of the yeare and diverse other things."[2] Also were they shown many and marvellous things pertaining to the harmony of the heavenly spheres. Then did they drink the mixed draught, the comfortable potation, joyously, philosophically, and with discernment, for at last had they attained to the divine Secrets of the Philosophers, even unto the mystagorical Delight, the great Fulfilment of the Spagyrick Quest of devout Oromaniacs.

[1] *The New Atlantis.* F. Bacon. [2] *Ibid.*

FRAGMENT FROM A LOST MS.,

PROBABLY BY ARISTOTLE, ENTITLED, περὶ ἀθλητικῆς, κ.τ.λ.; OR A TREATISE CONCERNING THE SPORTS AND PASTIMES OF THE ATHENIAN YOUTH WITH REGARD TO THEIR ETHICAL SIGNIFICANCE.

WE come now to investigate the position of the mountaineer, or climber of hills. Now, we may rightly call him the true mountaineer or climber of hills, who possesses the true love of mountain climbing, which, being a mean between two extremes, may be fitly termed a virtue. First, indeed, it is right to call the love of mountain climbing an active virtue, and not one of contemplation, for to no one is the ascent of a hill possible by contemplation alone; still, the virtue of a mountain climber is for a truth not wholly active, but is partly contemplative, as we shall show further on.

Moreover, the love of hill climbing, like fortitude or other virtues, has its defects, its mean, and its excess. Now, as we have said, virtue being a mean of which the extremes are the excess or the deficiency, he who is defective in this matter is one who either has not this love of climbing, or is indifferent in the matter; this man, indeed, is pitied by the hill climber, and indeed may be called the 'irrational man.' Now by the 'irrational man' we do not mean him who is unreasonable without qualification, but rather the man who is possessed of unreason from the point of view of the mountaineer, and truly amongst 'irrational men' are to be found the fathers of families, many learned men and others. Moreover, the 'irrational man' prefers rather to ascend hills by means of the telescope, or in a railway train, and if interrogated on the subject, expresses great scorn for those who rise at midnight, or in the early hours of the morning, for the purpose of imperilling their lives on the end of a rope. Again, he goes not to places where there are no hostels, alleging that he likes to be comfortable and enjoy himself. The scarcity of inns, however, in mountainous countries is a matter which, in these times, has in some few instances been remedied, for we are credibly informed that on the topmost summit of the lofty Mount Snowdon, in the Principality of Wales, an hostel exists, where the 'irrational man' may find gratification for his baser appetites, and perhaps may also at the same time experience, in a limited manner, that happiness which in its full degree is experienced by the true lover of hill climbing, whom we may call the 'mountaineer.'[1] Further, the 'irrational man' is inclined often to treat the adventures of the 'mountaineer' as travellers' tales, but in this respect he is unable rightly to distinguish between the true climber of hills and the 'pseudo-mountaineer' who haunts the smoking-rooms of certain hostels. This man climbs, but in imagination only. He will relate how he has ascended certain high and difficult, nay, even inaccessible peaks, and will brand the names of many hills on staves, that when he returns to his native land he may win much reverence. But although the 'pseudo-mountaineer' pretends to greater things than he has accomplished, and is, therefore, a depraved person, on the whole, perhaps, he appears more a vain than a bad man, for it is not for the sake of money that he would have the unwary traveller and the people of his nation believe his stories, but for the sake of honour and glory, which in itself is praiseworthy.

Now both the 'pseudo-mountaineer' and the 'irrational man' err by way of defect, being indifferent to the true joys of mountaineering. But the 'mountaineer' is he who has this virtue in the right measure. He delights not in climbing this

[1] The great Lexicographer defines the word as 'an inhabitant of the mountains, a savage, a freebooter, a rustick.' Can the word be here used in this sense?

hill or that, but in climbing itself. He loves to wander in mountainous lands; ascents of great mountains, clad in frozen snow, to him are not unprofitable. Mountain-huts ill-ventilated, nights spent under rocks, amidst snow, wind, mist, or rain, these things will he endure. Moreover, to help him, will he even pay much money to the more hardy inhabitants of the hills, who are able to guide him with skill and safety through the inhospitable fastnesses, which he loves to explore. Thus much knowledge will he gain, making observations on the heights of hills, the efficacy of meat lozenges, the movement of glaciers by day, and the *pulex irritans* by night. He is a searcher after sensations. But when, owing to misfortune, he finds that his desire for climbing is in inverse ratio to his opportunity for so doing, then will he spend his leisure hours in adorning his maps with red lines, or he will write papers, yea, even books, describing his former exploits, so that perchance other 'mountaineers' may receive benefit therefrom.

But, as we have already said, the love of mountain climbing, like fortitude and other virtues, has its mean and its defect; as to the mean, we have seen that it is the virtue of the 'mountaineer,' whilst the defect constitutes the habit of the 'pseudo mountaineer' and the 'irrational man.' But the extreme is found in the man who has the desire to climb hills out of all reason, therefore we call him the 'oromaniac,' or he who is incontinent in the matter. He it is who ascends hills on the wrong side, and cares not to travel in the line of least resistance; also should he hear that a pinnacle of rock is inaccessible, he is at once seized with a great desire to climb that pinnacle. For he climbs not mountains for the exercise, or the love of climbing itself, but for the mere base desire to beat all records or to outdo an enemy, or that he may see his name blazoned in the local papers. And not unfrequently do accidents befall such an one, and he hurts himself grievously; hence come those accidents which we may call indefinite, for of this kind of accident there is often no definite cause, for the cause of it is casual, and that is indefinite. Thus such an one may have fallen. Now if it was not his intention so to do, and he either slipped or was otherwise moved in a direction suddenly downwards, it happened accidentally. The accident, therefore was generated, and is, but not so far as itself is, but as something else is. Moreover, in this kind of accident, as we have already stated, it often happens that the 'oromaniac' suffers many woes; breaking sometimes a limb, or, if still more unfortunate, his neck, or he suffers mutilation[1] in respect to his garments. Again, accidents may be called that which is inherent to something, and of which something may be truly asserted; as for instance, if any one going up one mountain in a mist should, after much fatigue, find himself at the summit of another, the ascent would be an accident to him who climbs the mountain. Nor, if any one climbs one mountain, does he for the most part climb another. Accident is after another manner denominated, that which essentially belongs—'The inseparable,' for instance, the mountains themselves. Hence, indeed, it happens that accidents of this kind are perpetual, which is not the case with any others. Now concerning the love of mountain climbing, and the excess and deficiency thereof, as well as the mean which is also a virtue, and concerning also accidents both separable and inseparable of mountain climbing, let this suffice.

[1] Of the mutilated we have spoken elsewhere. 'A man is mutilated when some part is taken away, and this not any part indifferently, but which, when wholly taken away, cannot again be generated. Hence, men that are bald are not mutilated.'—*Metaphysics*, Book v. chap. xxvii.

10

NOTES ON THE HIMALAYAN MOUNTAINS

THE great flood of the Indus in 1841 seems to have been one of the most tremendous cataclysms recorded as having occurred on the continent of India. The exact reason of it was for many years unknown. Major Cunningham suggested that it was due to the bursting of an ice-dammed lake on the Shayok river. Major Becher seems, however, to have been the first who expressed a belief that it was caused by a landslip blocking the Indus near Gor. In a letter (*Journ. Asiat. Soc. Bengal*, vol. xxviii. p. 219) he writes that a mountain called Ultoo Kunn, near Gor, owing to an earthquake, subsided into the valley of the main Indus. Drew, in his book on Kashmir (p. 415), gives the following description: 'The flood of 1841 was in this wise. It occurred, as near as I can make out, in the beginning of June of that year. At Atak, a place twelve or fifteen miles below where the latitude-parallel of 34° crosses the Indus, the river had been observed during several months, indeed from December of the previous year onwards, to be unusually low; in the spring it had risen a little from the snow melting, but only a little, so that at the end of May (when in ordinary years the volume has greatly increased) it was still extraordinarily low. This in itself should have been enough to warn the people who dwelt by its banks, but so little was it thought of that a portion of the Sikh army was encamped on the low plain of Chach which bordered the river. One day in the beginning of June, at two in the afternoon, the waters were seen by those who were there encamped to be coming upon them, down the various channels, and to be swelling out of these to overspread the plain in a dark, muddy mass, which swept everything before it. The camp was completely overwhelmed; five hundred soldiers at once perished; only those who were within near reach of the hill-sides could hope for safety. Neither trees nor houses could avail to keep those surprised in the plain out of the power of the flood, for trees and houses themselves were swept away; every trace of cultivation was effaced; and the tents, the baggage, and the artillery, all were involved in the ruin. The result was graphically described by a native eye-witness, whose words were, "As a woman with a wet towel sweeps away a legion of ants, so the river blotted out the army of the Raja."' Drew was probably the first to actually visit the place where the block occurred. And a villager from Gor pointed out to him the exact spot where the debris of the landslip blocked the river. These floods seem to be of somewhat frequent occurrence. In 1844 one came from the Tshkoman valley above Gilgit. In 1858 another did great damage at Naushahra. The Indus at Attock (Atak) on 10th August was very low. In the early morning it rose ten feet in two hours, and five hours later it had risen no less that fifty feet, and continued rising till it stood no less than ninety feet higher than in the morning. It is probable that this flood came from the Hunza valley.

Smaller floods in the narrow Himalayan valleys are of frequent occurrence. For instance at Tashing, in 1850, a large lake was formed in the Rupal nullah by the snout of the Tashing glacier crossing the valley till it was jammed against the rock wall on the opposite side, thus blocking the Rupal torrent. Probably this will again happen, for when we were there in 1895 the Tashing glacier had once more blocked the valley to the depth of at least 200 feet, the Rupal stream finding its way underneath the ice; should this passage become in any way stopped, a huge lake must at once form behind the glacier.

The extreme narrowness, and often the great depth, of many of these Himalayan valleys will always be favourable to the production of these floods. Should a landslip occur, or should a glacier, such as the Tashing glacier, block the valley, a flood must be the inevitable result. On the Indus there are many places where a dam might easily be formed. In the bend underneath Haramosh, at Lechre under Nanga Parbat, or further down below Chilas in that unknown country where the Indus begins to flow in a southerly direction. For there on the map the Indus is made to flow between two peaks, *not three miles apart*: one is marked 16,942 feet, and the other 15,250 feet, thus making the depth of this ravine over 12,000 feet.

LIST OF SOME OF THE MOUNTAINS IN THE HIMALAYA THAT ARE OVER 24,000 FEET IN HEIGHT

The following list of mountains that are more than 24,000 feet has been taken from various maps. It gives most of the peaks that have been trigonometrically measured, but probably there are at least as many more in those great mountain ranges, the Hindu Kush, the Mustagh, the Kuen Lun, and the Himalaya, that are over 24,000 feet high.

The next highest peak in the world outside Asia is Aconcagua, 23,393 feet high.

		Feet.
	Devadhunga, Gaurisanka, or Mt. Everest, in Nepaul,	29,002
	K^2 in the Mustagh range,	28,278
	Kanchenjunga (1), north peak in Sikkim,	28,156
	Kanchenjunga (2), south peak,	27,815
5	Makalu, S.E. of Devadhunga,	27,799
	Dhaolagiri (1), in Nepaul,	26,826
	Unnamed peak N.W. of Katmandu,	26,680
	Nanga Parbat, or Diama, in Kashmir,	26,629
	Unnamed peak N. of Pokra Nepaul	26,522
10	K^1 in the Mustagh range,	26,483
	Hidden peak in the Mustagh range,	26,470
	Gusherbrum (1), in the Mustagh range,	26,360
	Gosai Than, N.E. of Katmandu,	26,305
	Gusherbrum (2),	26,103
15	Unnamed, N. of Pokra Nepaul,	26,069
	Gusherbrum (3),	26,016
	Unnamed peak, N.W. Katmandu,	25,818
	Unnamed peak, N.W. Katmandu,	25,729
	Masherbrum (1), in the Mustagh range,	25,676

		Feet.
20	Nanda Devi (1), in Kumaon,	25,661
	Masherbrum (2),	25,660
	Nanga Parbat or Diama (2),	25,586
	Rakipushi, in Kashmir,	25,550
	Unnamed, N. of Hispar glacier, Mustagh range,	25,503
25	Unnamed, N. of Hispar glacier,	25,493
	Dhaolagiri (2),	25,456
	Ibi Gamin, or Kamet, in Kumaon,	25,443
	K^{10}, in the Mustagh range,	25,415
	Boiohagurdaonas (1), N.W. of Hunza,	25,370
30	Jannu, in Sikkim,	25,304
	K^{11} in the Mustagh range,	25,210
	Nubra peak (1), N. of Leh, Mustagh range,	25,183
	K^{6} in the Mustagh range, Chogolisa peak,	25,119
	Bride peak, Baltoro glacier, Mustagh range,	25,110
35	Dhaolagiri (3),	25,095
	Boiohagurdaonas (2),	25,050
	Unnamed, N. of Pokra Nepaul,	24,780
	Nubra Peak (2),	24,698
	Tirach Mir (1), N. of Chitral Hindu Kush,	24,611
40	Unnamed, near Rakipushi, Kashmir,	24,470
	Muz Tagh Ata, Pamirs,	24,400
	Nanda Devi (2) (Nanda Kot),	24,379
	K^{12} in the Mustagh range,	24,352
	Tirich Mir (2),	24,343
45	Unnamed, N. of Katmandu Nepaul,	24,313
	Haramosh, near Gilgit Kashmir,	24,270
	Boiohagurdaonas (3),	24,044
	Unnamed, S. of Devadhunga, Nepaul,	24,020
	Kabru, in Sikkim,	24,015
50	Chumaliri, in Bhutan,	24,000
	Aling Gangri, in Tibet,	24,000
	K^{9} in the Mustagh range,	24,000

LITERATURE DEALING WITH THE HIMALAYA

Bogle, G., Account of Tibet. Philosophical Transactions, No. 67, part 2, and Annual Register, 1778.

Turner, Capt. S., Account of an Embassy to the Court of the Teshoo Lama, in Tibet, 1 vol., 1806.

Webb and Raper, Journey to explore the sources of the Ganges. Asiatic Researches, vol. x.

Colebrooke, H., On the height of the Himala Mountains. Asiatic Researches, vol. xi.

Moorcroft, W., Journey to the Lake Mánasarówara. Asiatic Researches, vol. xii.

Kirkpatrick, Col. W., An Account of the Kingdom of Nepaul, 1 vol., 1811.

Hamilton, Francis, M.D., An Account of the Kingdom of Nepal, 1 vol., 1819.

Fraser, J. B., Tour through part of the Snowy Range of the Himālā Mountains, 1 vol., 1820.

Hodgson, B. H., Essays on Nepál and Tibet, etc., 2 vols., 1874; also no less than 170 papers to various periodicals, chiefly the Journal of the Asiatic Society of Bengal. Cp. Report on the Mineralogical Survey of the Himala Mountains. J. A. S. B. xi., part 1, p. x.

Vigne, G. T., Travels in Cashmir, Ladak, etc., 2 vols., 1835.

Thomson, T., M.D., Western Himalaya and Tibet, 1 vol., 1852.

Moorcroft, W. and G. Trebeck, Travels in the Himalayan Provinces, etc., 2 vols., 1841.

Gerard, Capt. A., Account of Koonawur, in the Himalaya, 1 vol., 1841.

Gerard and Lloyd, Tours in the Himalaya, 2 vols., 1840.

Cunningham, Sir A., Ladák, Physical, Statistical, and Historical, 1 vol., 1854.

Strachey, R., Physical Geography of Kumaon and Gurhwal and the adjoining parts of Tibet. R. G. S. Journal, xxi., p. 57.

Strachey, Capt. H., Physical Geography of Western Tibet. R. G. S. Journal, xxiii., p. 2, published separately, 1 vol., 1854; also Journey to Lake Mánasarówar, 1 vol., 1848.

'Mountaineer' (Wilson), A Summer Ramble in the Himalayas and Cashmere, 1 vol., 1860.

Hooker, Sir J. D., Himalayan Journals, 2 vols., 1854.

Saunders, Trelawny W., Sketch of the Mountains and River Basins of India, in two maps, with explanatory memoirs. Geographical Department, India Office, 1870.

Gordon, Lieut.-Col. T. E., The Roof of the World, 1 vol., 1876.

Wilson, Andrew, The Abode of Snow, 1 vol., 1875.

Indian Alps and How we Crossed Them. By a Lady Pioneer, 1 vol., 1876.

Markham, Clements R., A Memoir on the Indian Surveys, 1 vol., 1871; 2nd ed., 1878.

Montgomerie, Major T. G., Reports on the Trans-Himalayan Explorations, 1865-1867, 1869, and 1871 (Indian Survey).

Shaw, R., Visits to High Tartary, Yârkand, and Kâshgar, 1 vol., 1871.

Torrens, Lieut.-Col. H. D., Travels in Lâdak, Tartary, and Kashmir, 1 vol., 1862.

Bellew, Dr. H. W., Kashmir and Kashgar, 1 vol., 1875.

Drew, F., Jummoo and Kashmir Territories, 1 vol., 1875.

Bogle, G., and T. Manning, Narratives of their Journeys to Tibet and Lhasa, edited by Clements R. Markham, 1 vol., 1876.

Godwin-Austen, Col. H. H., Royal Geographical Society Journal, vol. xxxiv., p. 19.

Knight, Capt., Diary of a Pedestrian in Cashmere and Tibet, 1 vol., 1863.

Schlagintweit, H. and B., The Last Journeys and Death of Adolph Schlagintweit, 1854.

Conway, Sir W. M., Climbing in the Karakoram Himalayas, 1 vol., 1894.

Knight, E. F., Where Three Empires Meet, 1 vol., 1893.

MacCormick, A. D., An Artist in the Himalayas, 1 vol., 1895.

Waddell, L. A., Among the Himalayas, 1 vol., 1899.

Younghusband, F. E., The Heart of a Continent, 1 vol., 1896.

Boeck, K., Indische Gletcherfahrten, 1900.

Deasy, H. H. P., In Tibet and Chinese Turkestan, 1 vol., 1901.

Durand, A., Making of a Frontier, 1 vol., 1900.

Holdich, Col. Sir T. H., Indian Borderland, 1 vol., 1901.

Bose, P. N., Glaciers of Kabru, 1 vol., 1901.

Workman, Mrs. F. B. and Dr. W. H., In the Ice-World of Himalaya, 1 vol., 1900.

INDEX